# The Parchmore Partnership

# The Parchmore Partnership

George Lovell, Garth Rogers
and Peter Sharrocks

Edited by Malcolm Grundy

Chester House Publications
2 Chester House, Pages Lane, London N10 1PR

First Published September 1995

ISBN 0 7150 0094 2

Printed by Clifford Frost Ltd., Wimbledon, London SW19 2SE

# CONTENTS

# INTRODUCTION

*Malcolm Grundy*

This is probably a unique story. The Parchmore Road Methodist church in Croydon, South London, has had three consecutive ministers who have attempted to develop the life of this local congregation by using consistent methods and policies. It is much more characteristic of any denomination that a new minister or priest will cut across the working methods of a predecessor. Sometimes this is desperately necessary. Often it only serves to frustrate those who have worked to support what seemed like agreed ideas. Such policy changes encourage a cult of personality around a minister rather than the idea of a minister as servant or enabler in a collaborative exercise.

This book encourages us to see how much more can be achieved when consistent working practices are employed. The Revd Dr George Lovell went to Parchmore in 1966 when it had just been designated as one of the 'Ten Centre' churches within the Methodist Connexion. These traditionally constructed chapels were to be developed into places where a range of community activities would be encouraged. The buildings and their congregations were to have a quite deliberate policy of service to the community offering facilities and services in co-operation with local authorities and other voluntary agencies. George Lovell came into contact with Dr T R Batten and his wife who offered a course at London University in community development. T R Batten had pioneered his working methods in Africa and, at that time, his programme was for students from developing countries. George Lovell took the course and began to apply the concepts of non-directive community development work at Parchmore. In the first section of this book he tells the story of how the work was begun. George went on to become the co-founder of Avec, a training agency devoted to bringing these principles more fully into the mainstream of congregational and ministerial life.

The Revd Garth Rogers followed as minister from 1972–77. He inherited policies and programmes which had been begun by George Lovell. His considerable organizational ability brought consolidation and continuity of policy rather than the traditional 'about turn'. He writes graphically and movingly about the youth culture of the day and the tense multi-cultural nature of the work.

The longest time of ministry at Parchmore is described by the Revd Peter Sharrocks who worked there from 1977–1989. He is quite definitely of the next generation of ministers. He carries little of the traditional clericalism of the Methodist minister nor the deference to the culture or apparent bureaucracy of that denomination. He was minister at a time when relationships with local authorities had to be re-negotiated and at a time when the children of immigrant groups needed to establish their own identity. A measure of the effectiveness of the Parchmore ministry through these three men is the way in which relationships with the police and the local community were maintained through more than twenty years of tension and change.

This is a revealing Christian story. It is a considerable achievement that time has been found to write about this work. The three ministers remain friends and colleagues and have co-operated in the production of the text. The Methodist Church has thought it right to make this story known and to give some financial assistance. The lessons which can be learned from this consistent piece of work are many and in the remainder of this introduction I want to highlight some of them. They are lessons and stories of achievement which are of importance for all those who are involved in ministry through the work of a local church. Needless to say the strategic lessons for those who devise policies and make clerical appointments are even greater.

## A STORY OF CHURCH AND COMMUNITY RELATIONS

The existence of groups and activities in a neighbourhood imply a relationship. If that relationship is a negative one of non-communication or non-involvement that absence of a relationship is also significant. There are churches, often now called 'associational' who do not want any real engagement with their local community and who, at the most, see it as a fishing ground for converts.

Parchmore is the reverse of this. Its members set out to have a deliberate policy of engagement with the community. In doing so a whole series of relationships are sparked into existence – with the young in various sub-groups, with pensioners, with local authority departments and employees, with the health care agencies and with other voluntary groups. There are certainly many others.

These are only relationships which can be described at surface level. A local congregation and its minister actively participating in community life also provokes a range of inner feelings, hardly understood or recognized by outsiders. Church brings memories of childhood, church means feelings of guilt, church means authority, church means patronizing charity, church means proselytizing and a hidden conversion agenda. All these unrecognized fears had to be overcome as the Parchmore work unfolded.

A consistent ministry of over twenty years gives a whole range of positive experiences remembered by individuals and by a community. It now means Parchmore is held in a trustful respect. A measure of this is that many outside groups come to the Christian Parchmore to mark significant events in their life. Church and community is about a reciprocal relationship.

## SYSTEMATIC CO-OPERATION WITH VOLUNTARY AND STATUTORY AGENCIES.

A great failing of the local church is to want to 'go it alone'. Often local Christian communities are not integrated into the life of their neighbourhood. They see other voluntary agencies as rivals who may well want to take their member's time away from vital church activities. They see local authorities as places where funds can be attracted or where the blame for lack of care can be placed.

The Parchmore story describes how relationships can be built up, very gradually, and over a long period of time. One basic community development method demonstrated at Parchmore is the need to work alongside other people and groups if lasting progress is to be made.

Each minister, after spending, listening, and negotiating time with the congregation, has set out to develop the building as a place where other community groups, and people of other faiths, can have their own identity and where they can co-operate in service to the community.

In the early days of Parchmore as one of the 'Ten Centre' churches it was hoped that funding would become available from National and local government. There was a moratorium but when this was lifted the funds were available. What we experience is the description of how a voluntary–statutory partnership can still exist, and be developed, when services are being cut back and when past expectations of welfare provision have to be re-evaluated. Partnership of a new kind has to emerge based on trust and new working relationships painstakingly established and maintained.

## COMMUNITY RESPECT AND A FAITHFUL CHURCH

Perhaps the most common characteristic of community life in inner-city and urban areas is the experience of frustration and disappointment. Family relationships are often under great strain. Promises made cannot be kept. Many ambitious schemes for youth work founder when money runs out or when a leader leaves. Attempts to develop trust with the police collapse when there is a local incident or when policy changes.

At Parchmore promises have been kept. Because care schemes and the open use of buildings has been maintained two or three generations have come to believe that Parchmore will deliver. Sudden about-turns have not happened. Quite the opposite, people have been encouraged to take more responsibility for their share in the Parchmore partnership.

An achievement like this can be written about and described. It has to be experienced by those living in comparative hardship before the real truth of this commitment can be known and understood.

## LEARNING FROM THE PARCHMORE EXPERIENCE

- Listening gains trust. Commitment pays dividends. It often feels like the 'long way round' but patient listening is the only way for genuine respect and participation to be achieved.
- Moving forward together is possible and prevents friction. The different groups and factions within a church have to co-exist in an atmosphere and within a structure which allows them to communicate, and negotiate, with one another.
- All-age integration is a must. Provision exclusively for one group in a church or a community produces an imbalance. People from different age groups and different backgrounds

need to feel that the church is offering a place where they can achieve equal respect.

- Racial harmony requires safety won through many years of difficulty in community relations. Parchmore has established a position of trust where the building can be regarded as a 'safe house' for those under threat.
- Reflection on experience is essential. Because it has been possible to discuss and analyse the many controversies and conflicts within Parchmore, learning through reflection and practice has become central and important.
- The use of an outside consultant is important. The role of T R Batten in the early days of George Lovell's ministry shows how much the understanding of a situation can be deepened by a skilled external reference point. Each subsequent minister has developed an important outside consultancy relationship in their own way. It is unlikely that the learning aspect of the Parchmore experience could have been done without the skills of outside consultants.

## SPIN-OFF FOR THE WIDER CHURCH

- The concept of non-directive work in a community setting has been established. The principle of working *with* rather than *for* people is now the core of all good community work practice.
- The understanding of how adults learn is demonstrated. Adults bring their experience of life to any new situation. Respect for their life story and reflection on current situations brings new learning which can then develop into action.
- The establishment of Avec. This community development training agency, simply meaning 'with', founded in 1976 by George Lovell and Catherine Widdicombe has enabled the good practice developed through Parchmore and T R Batten to be brought into the life of all the principal Christian denominations.
- Community work has developed into an independent discipline. The pioneering work done at Parchmore is acknowledged as a major contribution to the growing body of knowledge which informs community work training today.

THE STORY OF AN EXPERIMENT

This is the story of what can be achieved in religious and in social terms by a consistent policy to establish and develop a communal church. It shows that short ministries, if they are part of a strategic plan, can be effective. George Lovell was only at Parchmore for six years and Garth Rogers for five.

In some ways reading these stories is a historic time capsule. We will surprise ourselves that only thirty years ago we thought it enlightened to behave in particular ways. Hindsight and history can be both illuminating and cruel.

For me the most important impression of the years at Parchmore with these ministers is of the Lord walking with a people. They dialogue together and in doing so discover appropriate ways of service and of sharing faith with those who must be free to make their own journey.

# THE PARCHMORE MINISTERS AND AUTHORS OF THIS BOOK

**Revd Dr George Lovell, minister 1966-72** has been a circuit minister at Llanelly and Carmarthen, in Sydenham and Forest Hill and in Croydon. From 1970-75 he was engaged in an action research project designed to explore the implications of churches becoming involved in community development. From this work, with Catherine Widdicombe, he went on in 1976, to begin Avec, a service agency for church and community work. In 1991 he became Research Worker for Avec. George Lovell is the author of several books and numerous articles on church-based community development work. He is now a part-time minister in the Victoria and Chelsea Circuit and a Senior Research Fellow at Westminster College, Oxford.

**Revd Garth Rogers, minister 1972-77** began his ministry at the Coventry Methodist Mission. Before going to Parchmore he worked at the Manor Methodist Church in Bermondsey as part of the South London Mission. He went on to become minister and then Superintendent of the Manchester and Salford Mission where he was responsible for a major restructuring and devolution of the work. He is now Chairman of the London North-West District and lives in Hertfordshire.

**Revd Peter Sharrocks, minister 1977-89** became a Methodist minister after serving an apprenticeship as a draughtsman in the North-East of England. After training at Handsworth College he was sent to Dudley and then Bilston in the West Midlands. It was his appointment to the new town of Telford as the Churches' Youth Worker which thrust him into neighbourhood youth and community work and a ministry alongside people. After six years Peter was invited to become minister at Parchmore, where he was also able to develop work as a trainer of community and youth workers. Twelve years later he became Superintendent of the Wembley Methodist circuit, an appointment which was cut short by a call to become Superintendent of the Battersea Central Mission. In addition Peter has been Chairperson of the Churches' Community Work Alliance management committee and is an accredited Training Associate of Avec.

# ACKNOWLEDGEMENTS

I would like to thank the three principal authors of this book for their kindness in asking me to edit their writing. There have been times when I have had to be severe in cutting and adapting various sections of the text. This does not represent any criticism on my part of what has been written. Rather, it has served to increase my admiration for the rigour of the work which is being described. The thanks of all of us go to Valerie Tredinnick and May Farina for their work in typing the manuscript and to Catherine Ryan for helping us to order the material on our computer.

The London Committee of the Home Missions Division of the Methodist Church has been generous in giving financial support to the work, as has Avec in making its administrative resources available. We were delighted when Brian Sharp of the Methodist Church Division of Education and Youth agreed to become responsible for the publication of this book.

Very many people have been involved in the work at Parchmore alongside these three ministers. Some may be surprised and pleased to see their names mentioned, others will be disappointed to be left out. We can only apologize if an appropriate reference has not been given. Particularly in George Lovell's section, he would want to say that his writing style has not been to mention a large number of names but rather to describe and analyse events.

Most important for the authors is that these stories will do more than revive memories. It is our hope that readers will be spurred on to further service and learning and that the denominations will gain from this pioneering piece of church and community work an understanding of the advantages of strategic planning and consistent, skilled, ministerial appointments.

*September 1995*
*Malcolm Grundy*

# SETTING THE SCENE

*Peter Sharrocks*

## THE PEOPLE AND THE PLACE

Thornton Heath is part of the outer London Borough of Croydon. It began as a village at the end of a railway line and became an early haven for commuters. Over the years it has grown into a densely populated area of around thirty thousand people. In spite of being swallowed up within the greater London sprawl and being part of the very large London Borough of Croydon, Thornton Heath has managed to keep an identity of its own.

There is a busy High Street where once many local shopkeepers thrived. In the period covered by this book a few remained; a traditional type butcher, a greengrocer with an almost artistic display of fruit and vegetables, a hardware shop with its wares on the pavement, and a gents and ladies clothes shop which provides a personal service and is always referred to by the family name. These are more reminders of the past than typical of the place now. Shops have given way to estate agents, building societies, banks and fast food outlets. The traffic flow has been increased to saturation level by the building of two very large supermarkets at opposite ends of the High Street.

Places like Thornton Heath have always been cosmopolitan. Over the years spanned by this book the population has become more and more multi-racial. Post-war immigrants from the Caribbean have moved from inner London areas like Brixton and Balham and bought their own houses. They have been joined by Asians from East Africa, and immigrants from Ghana, Sierra Leone and Nigeria, and by people from Pakistan, and India. There are also residents from Europe: Poles, Turks, Greeks and there is a significant Irish community. The influx of black and Asian people has been matched by the movement from the area of white professional families towards leafier suburbs.

House prices in the London area have rocketed, and whilst Thornton Heath was not the most desirable of places for aspiring young couples, it became one of the more affordable places. Unlike some of the inner London regions, it has not become gentrified, but a lot of the older small accommodation has been modernized by young couples making their first homes. The old large Victorian property has been, or is being, converted into flats or has become home to extended black or Asian families.

Thornton Heath also contains an inter-war council housing estate, not far from Parchmore. Croydon is a Tory dominated council and has pursued the selling of council houses enthusiastically. One of the results is that the housing estate has become a mixture of privately owned neatly kept suburban bargain buys, ordinary rented accommodation, and a few streets where families of multiple-stress live in ghetto-type enclosures.

There are a few small factories tucked away behind the houses providing jobs, but Thornton Heath is a place where people live rather than work. Every morning they migrate all over South London, into Croydon with its massive office blocks, into neighbouring boroughs or into the City itself, like a swarm of worker bees. In the evening they return. At dawn and in the evenings hospital ancillary workers and office cleaners sweep into action, many of these are black women. Unemployment is higher in the northern end of Croydon than in some other parts, but unemployment has not been the scourge in the south that it has been in the north of England. It has been significantly worse for black young people. However, wages can be low, and the cost of living high, and the cost of accommodation which is in such short supply, astronomical.

It can be seen from this sketch of Thornton Heath that over recent years there have been many changes. It is the description of a community in transition. What has not yet been said is that it is set within a borough which is dominated by the perspectives of white professionals living and working in very different environments. The south of Croydon verges on to the green belt, with a bracelet of golf courses, and ribbons of highly desirable residential avenues, and the occasional black professional face. There are prestigious schools, and open green spaces. By contrast Thornton Heath has lost half of its secondary schools in borough reorganization, and has hardly any green space at all. Public amenities are not plentiful. Thornton Heath still has its swimming baths and a library, but there are no purpose-built community centres or public sports facilities other than six tennis courts.

Churches have struggled to survive. They are traditional institutions which find change and transition very difficult to negotiate. Apart from the Roman Catholic Church, which serves one of the largest parishes in London, including a large Irish population, the churches which have survived have done so because of the influx of Christians from the West Indies and Africa.

Parchmore has done better than most. This is the story of how one Methodist church not only survived the rapid social change of its environment, but actually discovered a newness of life, faith and Christian presence as it journeyed through its own transition process.

## PARCHMORE METHODIST CHURCH YOUTH AND COMMUNITY CENTRE

Parchmore is situated in Parchmore Road, which is one of the main roads leading into one end of the Thornton Heath High Street. It is within three minutes walk of the railway station, and close to the conjunction of a number of bus routes. It has become well-known to those who are interested in Church and Community Work as a pioneer in its field. It is even more well-known in its local community and the Borough of Croydon as a hub of activity and care in Thornton Heath.

It is not a purpose-built centre, and the outside is a poor advertisement for all that happens inside. It was built in the heyday of Thornton Heath as a desirable commuter village in 1900, a typical Wesleyan preaching house, with a large central pulpit, choir and organ behind, and a gallery. Sunday School rooms and halls were added later. During its first fifty years it flourished as a suburban Methodist church led by a succession of distinguished and scholarly ministers. The congregation was never sheltered from modern scholarship, and was encouraged to respond to the needs of its local community, especially during the two world wars. There were many successful social clubs organized by the members, and a strong Boys' Brigade tradition. Those days are still remembered with some affection as being settled, happy and secure. By the end of the 'fifties and the early 'sixties the old order was rapidly changing and ageing, and what was happening at Parchmore was symptomatic of what was happening in the nation and the Church as a whole.

# IMPRESSIONS OF CHANGE IN A DECADE 1955–65

In the 1950s young people became a distinctive and identifiable social group. They registered their presence by adopting their own style of music and clothes. Gangs formed, and they clashed with each other in public places from time to time. Rock and Roll provided the strident musical form which expressed the new assertiveness. There was a great deal of concern amongst the adult population who called for some action to curb the excesses of youthful behaviour and to direct their energies into wholesome activities. The government response was the Albermarle Report which amongst other things advocated the development of a professional youth service, and a capital programme to build youth centres in co-operation with the voluntary sector.

In the early 1960s the British voters were told that they had never had it so good. This was a slogan which really meant, you have never been better off. The improvements in personal wealth, and the subsequent expansion in leisure provision and personal entertainment systems like television was matched by a falling away from churchgoing. Nearly all churches during the 'sixties shrank, and none more so than in areas like Thornton Heath, where not only were they affected by the change in the religious climate, but also by the departure of many churchgoing people to the outer suburbs.

In the realm of theology there was ferment too. John Robinson's *Honest to God* is perhaps the most well-known example of fresh thinking, but there were others too. One of the emphases to emerge was that of the servant church, phrases like, 'the world writes the agenda for the church' were around. Harvey Cox's *Secular City* sought to promote a dialogue between the new sciences of sociology and community studies with theology. The general effect of these things was to promote the idea that churches needed to develop lifestyles that were much more sensitive to what was happening in the world around them.

One response to the new situation facing the churches was the formation of the King's Cross Training Centre by the London Methodist Districts and the Methodist Association of Youth Clubs. It was formed to encourage and service the development of youth work in Methodist churches in the London area and one of its initiatives called The Ten Centre Project was to have a crucial impact upon Parchmore.

## TIME TO CHANGE

The Revd Norman Dawson left Parchmore to become chairman of the London South-East District in 1963. Through his preaching and leadership the congregation had been introduced to the newly emerging ideas about mission, especially in relation to the role of the church as servant in the community. The national concern about young people referred to earlier had been given sharp focus in Thornton Heath because of the Craig and Bentley murder trial. Both young men had local connections, and had been taught by members of Parchmore's congregation. The local churches had come together to start open youth club work in a local school.

The Revd John Mitchell succeeded Norman Dawson and inherited a church that had large premises, a shrinking congregation, and a lifestyle suited to a neighbourhood that had largely disappeared and was likely to go on changing. John was sensitive to the needs of young people, and had a young family of his own. He was socially committed and eager to make the church relevant to the age of the community. He was also faced with a congregation most of whom were still very much wedded to the virtues of suburban Methodism with its cocktail of friendship groups, taste for good sermons, commitment to good works, and support for overseas mission. They liked what they were and valued their tradition. Parchmore Methodist church not only met their spiritual needs, but provided a network of social groupings in which they found friendship, warmth and security. Here there was continuity with the past, memories of events and relationships which were part of the fabric of their lives. Power was largely in the hands of the trustees, a fairly small group to whom most of the congregation deferred.

The new minister could see the need for change, and confronted the church with facts as he saw them; that with a diminishing congregation and ever rising costs in large but ageing premises it was necessary to think about the future. This very pragmatic perspective was linked to wider concerns about the community and the churches' obligation to respond to the needs not only of young people but also of the elderly and the handicapped. He also took an opportunity to reconstitute the body of trustees so that it represented a wider range of opinion, and was less resistant to the changes that he believed were vital.

Meanwhile, the King's Cross Training Centre conceived a scheme through which a considered and carefully planned development of church-based youth and community work might be carried out in ten churches. They were looking for churches in which this programme could take place. Parchmore was clearly a possibility, set as it was in a neighbourhood typical of its kind, thinking about modernizing its buildings, and anxious to reach out to young people. Meetings between Parchmore and officers of the King's Cross Training Centre were held, and after a relatively short and concentrated period the Leaders and Trustees at Parchmore were persuaded to involve themselves in the change, to adapt their buildings to accommodate a youth centre, and to a partnership with local government which would mean that open youth work would be carried out at Parchmore for the next twenty-seven years. For their part, local government and national government funds would pay 75% of any building costs, and a full-time youth worker would be seconded to work at Parchmore.

What is evident in all of this is that social change, theological ferment, government action and the response of the Methodist Church to it, converge to create an almost unique opportunity. The Parchmore people did not realize how much they were leaping into the unknown. They made their decision in faith believing it to be the right one, but there would be times when they wondered about the wisdom of what they had done. The brief ministry of John Mitchell had introduced a new perception of what the Methodist Church in Thornton Heath should be doing, and set in motion the process of building conversion. The story now to be told is of what followed.

It is the story of one church working for change within itself, and for change in the community of which it is part over a period of twenty-three years.

It is the story as told by the three ministers who have in their own ways sought to integrate the insights and skills of community development within the day-to-day practice of Christian ministry.

It is a story of a church which has scattered seeds of love and signs of the Kingdom as leaven in the lives of generations of people, young and old, from very many countries.

This is a story which has been written in the hope that others may find in it some clues to the way in which local churches might more effectively translate the gospel into meaningful presence and effective action.

Princess Diana visited Parchmore in February 1982. Here she is chatting to members of the Pop-In.

The Local Authority provides transport for the housebound to the Luncheon Club and the Pop-In.

A Community Service.

Entertaining on the occasion of the Volunteers' Social evening. From left to right: Roger Hulford, Mick Peake and Peter Sharrocks.

Youth Workers Dan Rodney (left) and Alan Holdsworth (right) with competitors in the Youth Club pool competition.

Local Councillor and J.P. George Mitchell shakes hands with Youth Worker Silvan Eastmond with Christine Morrison (Community Worker) (right) looking on.

With the aid of grants from Help the Aged and Croydon Council a new minibus is added to Parchmore's resources.

The exterior of Parchmore as the builders move in.

The team in 1988. From left to right: Roger Hulford, Nicola Hill, Diana Morrison, Carol Dobbs, Andy Lyons and Peter Sharrocks.

A 'meals on legs' volunteer delivering hot meals to local housebound elderly people.

# Part One

## Laying foundations

*– The Ministry of the Revd Dr George Lovell,*
*1966–72*

ILLUSTRATIONS

**Display:**



**Figure:**

# INTRODUCTION: THOUGHTFUL ACTION

Parchmore broke new ground during my ministry by establishing a centre in which we worked *with* rather than *for* people in the church and in the community. This approach is at the heart of church and community development. It is commonplace now. Some churches in most denominations practise it. Throughout the sixties it was novel and daring. Very few people were committed to it. Many Christians viewed it with grave suspicion and censured those who adopted it. There were very few places in which the approach was being practised rigorously and, whilst there were some books on community development, there were none on church and community development. Consequently we had to work things out for ourselves by trial and error. In fact, as one of the Ten Centres, Parchmore was a pilot project through which we were enthusiastically pioneering a new movement which we saw to be full of promise. Experiencing all this was exciting, inspirational, challenging and at times frightening.

Not surprisingly, therefore, during my ministry at Parchmore, and particularly during the first part of it, we were looking closely and critically at the approaches we were adopting and the methods we were using. This is reflected in my story of Parchmore because it is an important part of it. It was my good fortune to attend a course on community development led by Dr T R Batten and Mrs M Batten and subsequently to have the consultancy help of Dr Batten, a leading expert in the field and at the time Reader in Community Development Studies in the University of London. And so the Battens feature prominently in my story.

A dominant and abiding impression of the six years that I was privileged to be the minister of Parchmore is of a people alive with thought that led to action aimed at promoting human and spiritual development in the church and the community. People of all ages from the church and the community were thinking, talking and acting together with me in ways in which none of us had done previously. We were thinking about what we were doing and why, what was going on around us and about each other's ideas. Our thinking was down-to-earth. It was about theory, theology and spirituality but it was not abstract because it was directed towards action. Some of this thinking was done in committees and other formal groups such as teach-ins and workshops. Much of it was informal and impromptu at the end of services of worship, during pastoral visits or standing around a car at the end of a meeting. The excitement and satisfaction of it was reward enough for all the mind-stretching hard work and the stress it induced.

During my ministry we had to think our way into two new areas of work: community work and open youth work. At the same time we had to rethink the traditional work in which Parchmore was engaged: worship, occasional offices and devotional meetings, church youth work and the Christian education programme. Then we had to think our way through all that was involved in integrating the new work with the traditional work to make it into a unified programme of church and community development. To work for development in each of these areas and through the total programme we had to:

- think out basic underlying concepts such as our beliefs, purposes, and approaches;
- prepare and train ourselves for the work;
- design, plan and carry out work programmes;
- tackle problems;
- monitor progress and evaluate what happened.

These activities take us to the heart of the Parchmore story. So I have opted to tell about my time there by describing significant events associated with them. I start with a chapter reconsidering the Ten Centre Scheme and end with one on my reflections and a postscript. Then, in between, there are chapters on each of the activities. I can write in this way because we had to concentrate on one or other of the activities at different times even though they overlap and interrelate. We were, for instance, learning from all of them, not simply from the training sessions we had. Thinking out basic concepts was essential to all the other activities. I have drawn heavily upon records we made of our discussions and all that happened and various things I have written about them.

People of all ages from the church, the community and other organizations became involved in all these activities with the full backing of the church leaders. It happened like this. At the time the members of the Leader's Meeting had overall responsibility for the life and work of the church. They became distressed because they said that they simply had not the knowledge nor the experience to be responsible for the new programme of church, youth and community work.

Many of them felt that they had no alternative but to resign. They became leaders to undertake responsibility for the traditional church work for which they felt capable and which they enjoyed. Their job as they saw it was to give a lead but they felt they were no longer equipped to do so. Over a period of months I worked through the issues with them. Eventually they saw that whilst they themselves could not do all the thinking that had to be done they could make arrangements for others to do some of it with or for them. They realized that was a legitimate way to exercise their leadership. They were greatly relieved and gave themselves to making the necessary arrangements through teach-ins, workshops, conferences and working parties. In this way they helped to get anyone and everyone thinking things through. What normally happened was that the leaders authorized or commissioned work to be done. Sometimes they would ask for recommendations, sometimes they would make decisions with those involved and at times they would delegate responsibility with a clear remit. To do this they had to learn how to work with a lot of people and groups some of whom had very different lifestyles and values from their own. These procedures maximized participation, located the thinking in the area of concern, engendered interdependence and avoided Parchmore being controlled by an elite or a cabal as it had been in the past. At the same time it prevented the fragmentation of the life and work of the Centre by drawing people together in a common endeavour directed to Parchmore and all its enterprises. This entirely new way of working for the leaders was very successful.

An important part of my job was to promote, cultivate and service all those engaged in the activities listed above. Monitoring and researching what happened as objectively as possible helped me to do this, to raise questions and to provide information. I learnt much about how to do this through the action research which constituted my doctoral studies.

What I have done in my part of this book is to tell stories associated with critical events which illustrate the interplay between thought and action in Parchmore. Inevitably this has involved selecting those events and stories which readily illustrate the themes I have pursued. Sadly this means many important stories had to be left untold. I then reflect on their significance for me as a minister and for church and community development to which some twenty-seven years later I remain committed. The sequence in which I have told the stories is not strictly in the order in which the events occurred. So, before turning to them, I give an overall picture of my six years at Parchmore and set the events in chronological order.

During my ministry at Parchmore there were four main phases. The first phase was rethinking being one of the Ten Centres and then preparing and training ourselves to get on with it. (Roughly from October 1966 to July 1967.) The second phase was establishing church youth work, a comprehensive programme of Christian education and a programme of open youth and community work. To do that we had to work hard at theory and practice, theology and purposes. We were engaged in this throughout but strenuously so from September 1967 to August 1969. The third phase was re-organizing the administrative and executive structure of Parchmore. This phase overlapped the second, it was from the summer of 1968 to May 1970. The fourth phase, 1970 to 1972, was consolidating the work done, weaving together the old and new work programmes and introducing some new organizational structures. Also it was a time of preparing for my withdrawal, finding a successor and preparing for his ministry which for the first time was done in consultation and co-operation with people representative of all aspects of Parchmore's life.

The events about which I tell stories fit into these phases in the following way. So that you can look them up easily I have give the numbers of the pages where they can be found:

**Phase One: Rethinking and Training**
*The Society Meeting*, October 1966 (cf p13)
*The Teach-In*, February 1967 (cf p13f)
*The Battens' Course*, April–June 1967 (pp12f, and 15–21)

**Phase Two: Establishing a Comprehensive Work Programme**
*The Parchmore Workshop*, September–December 1967.
(cf pp31ff)
*Crisis about Crockery and Allocating Premises*, December 1967.
(pp 50ff)

*Appointment of the First Full Time Youth Worker*, February 1968. (p14f)
*Meeting Retired Peoples' Needs*, February 1968 onwards (pp 36ff)
*In Community, Sunbury Residential Conference*, March 1968 (cf pp 24ff)
*Rehabilitation of Ex-Mental Health Patients*, April 1968. (pp 39ff)
*Opening the New Centre*, 8th May 1968. (p21)
*The inauguration of a comprehensive Christian education Programme*, October 1968. (cf pp43ff)
*Aggressive behaviour in the youth centre: The November crisis* 1968. (cf pp53ff)
*Community Groups; Sunbury Residential Conference*, March 1969. (cf pp63ff)
*The Inauguration of a More Comprehensive Programme of Worship*, April–November 1969. (cf 67ff)

**Phase Three: Reorganizing the Administration**
*The inauguration of the Parchmore Church Youth and Community Council*, May 1970. (cf pp46ff)

**Phase Four: Consolidating and Withdrawing**
*The Teach-In*, March 1971. (cf pp33f, 48f)
*My Withdrawal*, August 1972. (cf p79f)

# — Chapter One —
# BECOMING ONE OF THE TEN CENTRES

## THE INITIAL WORKING SITUATION

My ministry at Parchmore started in September 1966. I had accepted gladly the invitation to work with the people in making their church into one of the Ten Centres. The intention that I should start my ministry in the remodelled premises was thwarted by a moratorium imposed by the Department of Education and Science on all such schemes as part of an economy drive. In fact when I started my ministry the plans for making Parchmore into one of the centres was in abeyance.

Conflicts and tensions generated by the Ten Centre scheme were dormant but unresolved. Some people were passionately in favour of the scheme. Others were equally passionately against it. A small majority of the trustees and leaders voted in favour of it. Most people felt that the scheme had been imposed upon them, that they had been allowed little real say in whether or not Parchmore should become one of the Ten Centres and that their warnings about the difficulties of controlling local young people in clubs had been disregarded by the advocates of the project. They were angry about this. Some people saw it as a way of providing better premises for open youth work, church organizations and for worship. Some welcomed the breadth of the religious and secular provision because they saw it as an expression of their faith; others saw the open youth work as a penalty to be paid for a new church. Some saw it as a way to provide people in the local community with care, services and resources without strings. Others said that the scheme was in essence a major evangelical venture, a way to reverse the decline in church membership. For some it was entirely a local scheme, but for others it was part of a wider movement. Underlying this free market of aims were the conflicting ideologies and theologies from which they were derived.

As I was not held responsible for initiating the scheme I was not the object of the aggression reserved for those who had started it all. In fact, I was the recipient of a considerable amount of sympathy. People were sorry, concerned and apologetic about what they considered to be an enormous and difficult task that I had inherited! By default, not design, I was in a strong position from which to work with all the people. I felt I had been given a glorious opportunity. I had never ministered in a situation with so many people and resources. The church had a great history and I was confident that the scheme presented a practical way in which to fulfil part of the mission of the local church in Thornton Heath providing, that is, the people came to really want it. I was very happy to be at Parchmore.

Within a very short time of my arrival I was convinced that I must establish myself as a minister acceptable to all the Parchmore people, I simply had to become their minister. So I concentrated on them, their personal needs and the groups and organizations that were important to them. I was at pains to accept them as they were and to offer my support. I took everyone's part and avoided taking sides. They knew I was for the scheme because I had been invited to be the minister to it. I was at pains to make clear in public and private that people had a right to their viewpoint and that they had a responsibility to raise any concerns they might have: they and their concerns simply had to be considered thoroughly in love if we were to find our way forward together and achieve our objectives for people in the church and the community. Therefore, I did all I could to see that all positions and points were taken seriously. One of the results was that I found myself deeply involved in pastoral conversations with individuals and groups about their feelings about Parchmore and the scheme to make it a church, youth and community centre.

I soon realized that the people as well as the leaders and trustees needed an opportunity to reconsider the scheme freely, openly, critically and constructively with me and with each other. I was convinced that its success depended upon all the people connected with Parchmore being given an opportunity to do this in relation to some hard facts which concerned me. There was no one in Parchmore, for instance, willing to do open or closed youth work; there were strong feelings against the young people who had attended the clubs on Parchmore premises; the committees responsible for the youth work had not met for more than eighteen months. All the church work with children and young people was very weak apart from the Boys' Brigade. There was no experience of community work. Providentially the moratorium made it possible to reconsider the project. Decisions had been made and grants negotiated but the building contracts had not been signed. We could still withdraw from the Ten Centre scheme and the government offer of grant aid. Inwardly I had come to see that I would accept a local decision to withdraw although I would not have found it easy to do so. To withdraw from remodelling the premises need not necessarily have been the end of the church and community development project. It would have removed one of the main objections to the scheme, dismantling the beloved and beautiful chapel. Indeed, it could have paved the way for the people to design their own church and community development programme. Youth and community work could have been developed without any modification to the premises. What I was not prepared to do, however, was to abandon my commitment to church and community development and that was why I wanted everyone to have a say in deciding for or against the scheme.

Considering what training we all needed in church and community development work was an important part of making a decision. Eight years of experience as a Methodist minister had proved to me that I simply had to learn new ways of working with people if I was to tackle this new job with any confidence and hope of success. So as part of my preparation for my ministry at Parchmore I had set out to find appropriate training. I wrote to many different people describing the problems.[(1)] Hope and help came from Dr T R Batten. A letter I wrote to the University about my needs and problems arrived on his desk. He rang me suggesting we meet after I had read his books. We met, and almost immediately we were immersed in one of the most exciting discussions I have ever had. As we constructed and pored over diagrams and charts about my situation I knew intuitively and conclusively that I had found someone who could help me to find what I was looking for. I was convinced that he had discovered, researched and tested out ways of getting people to think and work things out for themselves which respected their autonomy. I could see that they would be successful in the situations in which I had failed to do just that. I left his room in Woburn Square in great excitement and anticipation. I had found the key for which, unknowingly, I had searched; it is frequently described as the non-directive approach to working with individuals and groups. I began to see that my previous way of working with people was a dysfunctional combination of elements from democratic methods, directive approaches and laissez faire attitudes.[(2)] Dr Batten offered me a place on a full-time three-months course in the summer term 1967 conditional upon my having the permission of the Parchmore people to attend it. It was necessary to make an early decision about this possibility.

## OPTING TO BE A CENTRE FOR COMMUNITY DEVELOPMENT

A society meeting had been fixed for the Autumn. This meeting was open to all officers, members and adherents. It was extremely well attended. As I felt widespread acceptance by the people I introduced a discussion about the need to reconsider the scheme and to make decisions about our further training in the light of our conclusions. I suggested that a teach-in would enable us to look at just what church and community development is all about and to focus on working with people rather than on building work. This would help us to see what we were committing ourselves to and whether or not we wanted to do so. After thorough discussion the suggestion was accepted enthusiastically by those for and against the scheme and in the event representatives of both groups attended the teach-in. With the same kind of enthusiasm it was agreed that I should attend the course run by Dr T R and Mrs M Batten at the University of London. The members of the meeting said that they were sending me to learn new skills to use in Parchmore and to share with them. The story of the course is told in the next section. Together, I felt, we had begun to take another, and a different look at the scheme. For me this was a highly significant event. Expectancy and excitement were in the air. I was deeply moved. I felt, and I know others did, that a new era and movement had begun. The privilege of being part of it thrilled me and filled me with joy. The mood of the meeting said we were going to do something new together and we were glad to be doing it.

Over seventy people shared the Teach-In on a Saturday afternoon in February 1967, two months before I attended the Battens' course. A small group of people from one of the Ten Centres already established took part. We were soon disabused of any thought that they had come to tell us what to do. They had come to help us to think about our thoughts about becoming a centre in the light of their experience. The members of the teach-in willingly gave themselves to thinking things through for themselves and got out a range of questions under four headings: the nature of the church and its involvement in a Ten Centre scheme;

determining real local needs; staffing the youth and community work; and organizing and running the centre. It was an amazing experience to work on getting out the subjects on which we must work and work hard to make the building scheme into a community development project.

It was a very different experience from the previous discussions about the scheme: it simply had to be. It mirrored what I was beginning to glimmer about community development approaches. People explored ideas and problems rather than argued for or against propositions. What people thought mattered, and they were encouraged and enabled to share it. New ideas were introduced but not imposed indeed people realized that there were things that they had to decide for themselves. There was a freedom for thought in the air. For most of those present it was a first experience of a different way of working at things and they responded positively to it.

Gradually the scheme was taking a different shape in the minds of the Parchmore people. One person said, 'When we began we thought this scheme was about a building but now we see it is all about people'. Attention was focused upon church and community development rather than on a youth and community centre and a youth worker. Increasingly people liked what they learnt about the ideas underlying the project. They wanted to be involved in this kind of work whether or not the premises were remodelled. A strong tide of opinion was now running in favour of going ahead with becoming one of the Ten Centres when the moratorium was lifted. I felt we had overcome the faction, got a more profound understanding of what the scheme was all about and established a sounder basis upon which to build. I also felt that I had been properly mandated by the officers and the people to act as worker to the scheme.

Soon after the teach-in people freely decided to go ahead with the scheme. The moratorium was lifted. Government funds were made available towards the capital costs. Building contracts were signed, the church was vacated on Easter Sunday 1967. We had committed ourselves to study community development and to think out the fundamentals of our own programme whilst the building was being converted. In fact we too were being converted to new ways of working and organizing ourselves. A full-time youth worker, Miss Penny Thatcher, was appointed in February 1968, through the local authority.

And so I went on the Battens' course.

## FINDING HOW TO DO THE JOB

The Battens' course enabled me to experience and study the non-directive approach and to learn about community development in a group of thirteen people from eleven countries and five religions. We studied the theory, examined in detail how to be non-directive, practised the approach in the group, studied numerous cases and considered their implications for each of our work situations. Learning to be non-directive was difficult because the directive approach was so deeply ingrained in me. I had to make transformational changes in my ways of thinking and speaking about working with people and in my ways of planning and doing it. In fact, I had to change my mode of being.

What I learnt from the Battens fundamentally altered the course of my ministry. It was a conversion experience which led to a radical shift in the way in which I work with people in church and community. Before I met the Battens, I worked *for* people, now I work *with* them. I practised what I learnt from them assiduously throughout my six years at Parchmore. The incredible developments which occurred in and through Parchmore I attribute to the non-directive approach and I wrote a doctoral thesis to prove it.(3) It is incredible that such a negative sounding concept is packed with such positive dynamic development power, but it is. Parchmore proves it.

## THE NON-DIRECTIVE APPROACH

This non-directive way of doing and being must be described because it is so central to my ministry and to the Parchmore story. Continuous application and study of this approach for over twenty-seven years has refined my understanding and practice of it and informed and strengthened my commitment to it.(4) However in order to follow the story through I will describe how I understood the approach at the time. I can do this quite faithfully because what I thought is well documented by the Battens and by myself. Happily for me they published a very important book on the subject in 1967 whilst I was attending the course, *The Non-Directive Approach in Group and Community Work*.[5] They describe what a non-directive worker does in this way:

> The worker who uses the non-directive approach does not attempt to decide for people, or to lead, guide or persuade them to accept any of his own specific conclusions about what is good for them. He tries to get them to decide for themselves what their needs are; what, if anything, they are willing to do to meet them; and how they can best organize, plan and act to carry their project through. Thus he aims at stimulating a process of self-determination and self-help and he values it for all the potential learning experiences which participation in this process provides. He aims to encourage people to develop themselves, and it is by thinking and acting for themselves, he believes, that they are most likely to do so.[6]

For the Battens and for me this approach was the principal tool of community development. I have discussed it further in my Postscript.

## REASONS FOR ADOPTING THIS APPROACH

Before I could adopt the non-directive approach and the processes associated with community development I had to feel confident not only that they would work but that they were consistent with ideas and beliefs I held to be important. I felt I could commit myself as a Christian minister to them because they help people to form religious and secular communities based on loving relationships between people and God. Forming such communities I believe to be an important part of the Christian mission.[7] I develop this also in the Postscript.

## A DEVELOPMENT DESIGN FOR THE PARCHMORE PROJECT

Like the other members of the course, I had to prepare a paper about the work in which I was engaged. I worked hard at this and was feeling pleased with the third draft I submitted to Dr Batten. I was quite devastated when he said to me that he did not see anything of a development project in my paper! He said that the project as presented provided services for people and described it as a community care programme. The term has taken on a new meaning recently but he used it to indicate the patronage in the scheme, the doing good to others. He was right. I realized that it is one thing to use the non-directive approach in a group but quite another to write it into the design of a project as a pivot of development. I started again intent on producing a development project paper. Eventually it came together in me and on paper. I had the design of a development, rather than a building, scheme!

Establishing my purposes was the thing I found most difficult to do in preparing the paper although when I look at them now they seem so obvious. I remember getting up at 5am on several mornings over a period of two weeks to try to bring order out of my many thoughts. Attempt after attempt went into the waste paper basket but eventually I came up with the following:

- To assist as many people as possible in Thornton Heath to develop their personalities and to achieve status and significance both as individuals and in their relationships with each other and to care for each other.
- To help members of the church to work out in their daily lives in the community around them the principles inherent in their faith.
- To help people to realize their religious needs as wants and to find appropriate means of satisfaction.

The major problem was to sort out my primary purposes from my initial objectives and ways and means of achieving them which are reproduced in Display 1. Some of the objectives and ways and means started life as primary purposes.[8] This was certainly true of the first objective, to provide a centre by remodelling the church premises as a Church, Youth and Community Centre and of the third ways and and means, to provide new opportunities for social, physical and spiritual activities and satisfactions. Had these remained primary purposes, my attention would have been on buildings and satisfying activities as ends rather than as possible, but by no means automatic, means to the ends of human and spiritual well being and development. Getting out the primary purposes fixed my attention on the development of people, their relationships and their environment through the development of buildings, church and community work and religious and secular organizations, etc. This subtle but vital change of inward orientation formed me into a minister who is a development worker.

The rewards of differentiating my purposes from the other categories far outweighed the costs of doing so. For six years I used them over and over again to help me think things out, to plot the course of developments, to make decisions and to evaluate work done. Sorting out my purposes enabled me to get Parchmore people to determine their purposes in a fraction of the time I had given to the task. (*see Display 1 opposite*)

Phrasing purposes, objectives, ways and means so that they expressed essentials of the non-directive approach and community development processes, was also an important part of the business of writing a paper that represented a development project. They had to speak of participation, self-determination and self-development of people and workers, assisting people to do their own thing, stimulating, facilitating, enabling, empowering, working *with* rather than *for* people. The last point, essential to the scheme as a development project, I developed further in a diagram the basics of which are reproduced on p20, in Figure 1. It shows how workers from the church, other organizations and the community could work together in different settings and how people from the church and the community could enjoy joint membership of different clubs and activities. It broke with the tradition that the church must provide the leaders and workers and the community the members. This idea worked in practice. Gradually, but not without some difficulties and conflicts, workers and members from church and community mixed together on equal terms. This promoted the interrelated development of all kinds of people and of the church and a range of organizations and institutions.(9)

The paper also set out a workshop training programme which is described later; cf pp31ff. And it listed difficulties that I foresaw. Previously I would have hidden these from sight but now I was facing them and their implications.

**Objectives**

To provide a centre by remodelling the Church premises as a Church, Youth and Community Centre, with rooms for groups to meet in and a coffee bar open to all members of the centre and other, e.g. lonely, reserved, unattached and casual visitors, without any obligation to participate as a member of the Centre.

To staff the centre with

- a full-time professional youth worker;
- voluntary workers drawn from church membership, from other churches and local organizations;
- a full-time professional community development worker.

To train the voluntary staff.

- To work with unattached neighbourhood groups existing outside the centre.
- To draw together all those interested in the development of the local community for consultation and discussion.

**Ways and Means**

- By building on the existing church and community life centred on the Parchmore Road Methodist Church.
- By developing the life of the church and its ancillary organizations.
- By providing new opportunities for social, physical and spiritual activities and satisfactions.
- By stimulating those who join the centre to decide exactly what sort of a community centre life they want and helping them to get it within the limits imposed by the Trust Deeds of the Methodist Church which, for example, expressly forbid the supply, sale and use of intoxicants or any form of gambling on Methodist Trust Premises.
- By giving all groups (new and old, religious and non-religious) as much freedom for self-chosen activity and change as is consonant with the Constitutional Practice and Discipline of the Methodist Church.
- By encouraging church members to become members (not just workers) of the groups within the centre.
- By encouraging and training members of the church and centre to become members and workers in outside organizations.
- By being alive to the needs, wants and tensions of members and sections of the community and by being actively engaged with others in welfare and pastoral work to reduce and to relieve them.
- By helping people in the centre and community to discover and to make their contribution to the development and creation of the community life of the centre and neighbourhood.
- By setting up church and community training workshops.
- By organizing a counselling centre service.

**Display 1** My objectives and ways and means of achieving them

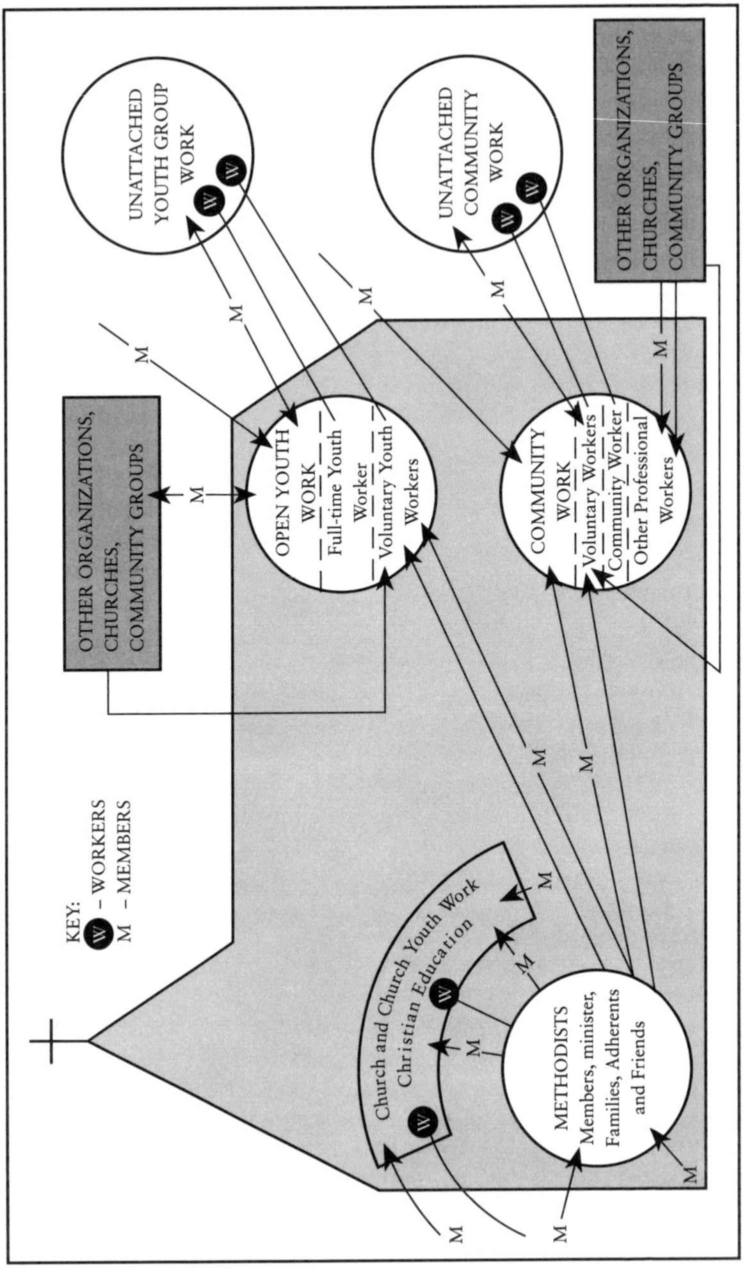


**Figure 1** Project design for Parchmore Church, Youth and Community Centre

The paper and the diagram described and illustrated essentials of the design of a development programme (Figure 1). It was a working brief which helped me to sort out my ideas in such a way that I was open to the ideas of others. It was private preparation for a non-directive programme of development work. I returned to it over and again.

## OPENING THE NEW CENTRE

Parchmore was crowded to capacity for the opening ceremony on the 8th May 1968. There was a service at which the late Revd Derek A Greaves preached. Derek had a distinguished ministry at Parchmore between 1947 and 1952 and was still much loved and admired. He spoke of the scheme as an experiment in establishing bridgeheads between those inside and outside the church. A telling metaphor as he had been a chaplain during the 1939–45 war to the parachute regiment and done many drops. He thought it would enable many people to serve the community. He saw Parchmore as a place in which the sacred and the secular would mingle. And he warned the church people against trying to communicate Christianity by ostentatiously talking about it. His presence at the ceremony and his commendation of the work helped many people to accept the changes.

This service was followed by tea and speeches. Mr Paul Bartlett Lang handed over a substantial cheque towards the costs of rebuilding on behalf of the Joseph Rank Benevolent Trust Fund. Then the youth centre opened its doors for the first time.

It was a marvellous occasion. Full of great promise. We were full of energy for the work that lay ahead of us.

# — Chapter Two —
# THINKING OUT BASIC UNDERLYING CONCEPTS

The three stories in this section illustrate the way in which throughout the six years we had to think and think again about basic concepts in order to do the work, to come to terms with each other and the developments and difficulties we experienced, and to survive.

**Purposes**

My experience of defining my purposes whilst on the Battens' course had been so valuable that I invited the members of the Workshop during their first session (September 1967) to define their purposes. Remembering the difficulties that I had experienced and the time I had taken to do this exercise for myself, I just did not know how to get them to do it in an hour or two. Eventually I hit upon the idea of using the *Voluntary Social Services Handbook and Directory*(1) to introduce the session rather than giving a talk about the importance of purposes. By reading selected entries I illustrated that each entry had the name of the organization, its 'objects' and the activities by which the organization intended to achieve them. It was readily agreed that it was important to have objects or aims (i.e. 'to know where you are going') and to differentiate between 'objects' and 'activities'. What I had not realized beforehand was that simply reading out the objects would of itself communicate immediately the importance and usefulness of being clear about them. The workshop members agreed to define their aims. They did this in randomly selected sub-groups as though they were preparing an entry for a directory by trying to answer the question: 'What are we trying to do by building and running a centre along with all the other things connected with the church?'

The groups reported back to a plenary session later in the evening. I listed their answers on blackboards. Time having run out, I got permission to sort and collate the profusion of points by way of preparation for the next meeting. I circulated my draft. After careful consideration the following statement was agreed:

**Aims**

- To be a living church working in the community as a practical example of Christianity.
- To help people in Thornton Heath to develop their lives to the full whether or not they become Christians in the process.
- To be involved in the life of the neighbourhood and the community and to involve them with us in our community project.
- To extend our working links with other churches in Thornton Heath.
- To overcome the prejudice against the church.

**Ways and Means**

- By creating a Church, Youth and Community Centre in which the church is the heart and the source of life and meaning.
- By gaining strength for the tasks by drawing upon spiritual resources through maintaining a strong worshipping community.
- By accepting all as equals who come to the Centre or Church.
- By determining and meeting community and individual needs in Thornton Heath in the name of Jesus Christ.
- By providing those outgoing services for the community which the church, but not the state, can provide.
- By communicating the Christian meaning of life through the manner in which people and their needs are served, and the Christian 'atmosphere' of the Centre.
- By caring for people physically, socially and spiritually.
- By contributing our knowledge towards the solving of personal and community problems.

These purposes were used throughout my ministry in relation to all that we did. It is not difficult to see how the work I had done on the Battens' course helped us to do this exercise. This is a good example of the effective combination of group and preparatory work.

**Beliefs**

In March 1968, some two months before the remodelled premises were opened, fifty-seven people spent a weekend in a conference centre in Sunbury to prepare for their new community role and to help them to face up to the implications of the changes taking place.(2) Twenty-two of them were between the ages of twelve and sixteen. The others represented all ages up to eighty. They all took active parts in the discussions. The title of the conference was, 'In Community'.

One of the things we considered was how we thought the church ought to relate to the world and how we in Parchmore ought to do so through the project. I used one of Hans Ruedi Weber's diagrams to get people modelling this relationship.(3) It is reproduced below in Figure 2. It represents Christian mission as an expedition into the world to bring people into the church and away from the world. Missioners move from the church into the world with the sole purpose of bringing people into the church. Members of the workshop found this concept unacceptable and objectionable, as indeed it was to me.

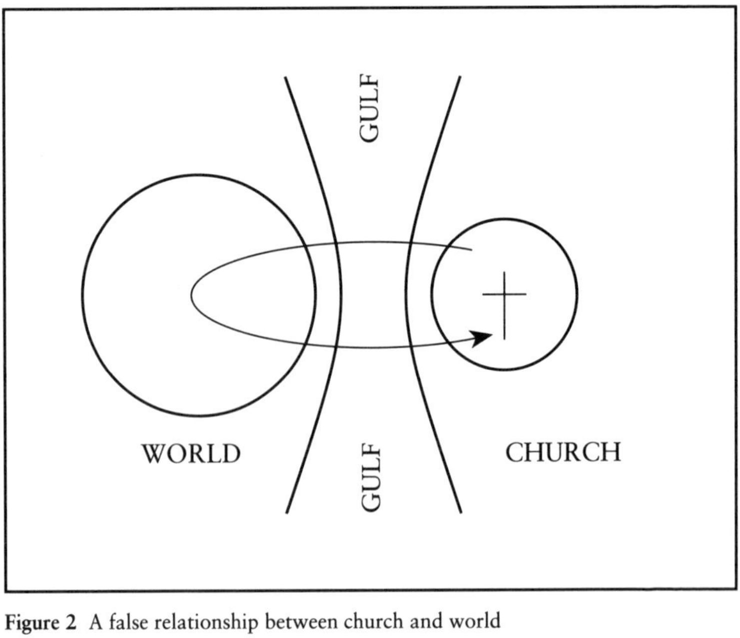


**Figure 2** A false relationship between church and world

Then children, young people and adults constructed diagrams representing what they understood to be the relationship between the church and the world and shared them. The result was an amazing range of diagrams. A selection of them is given in Figure 3.

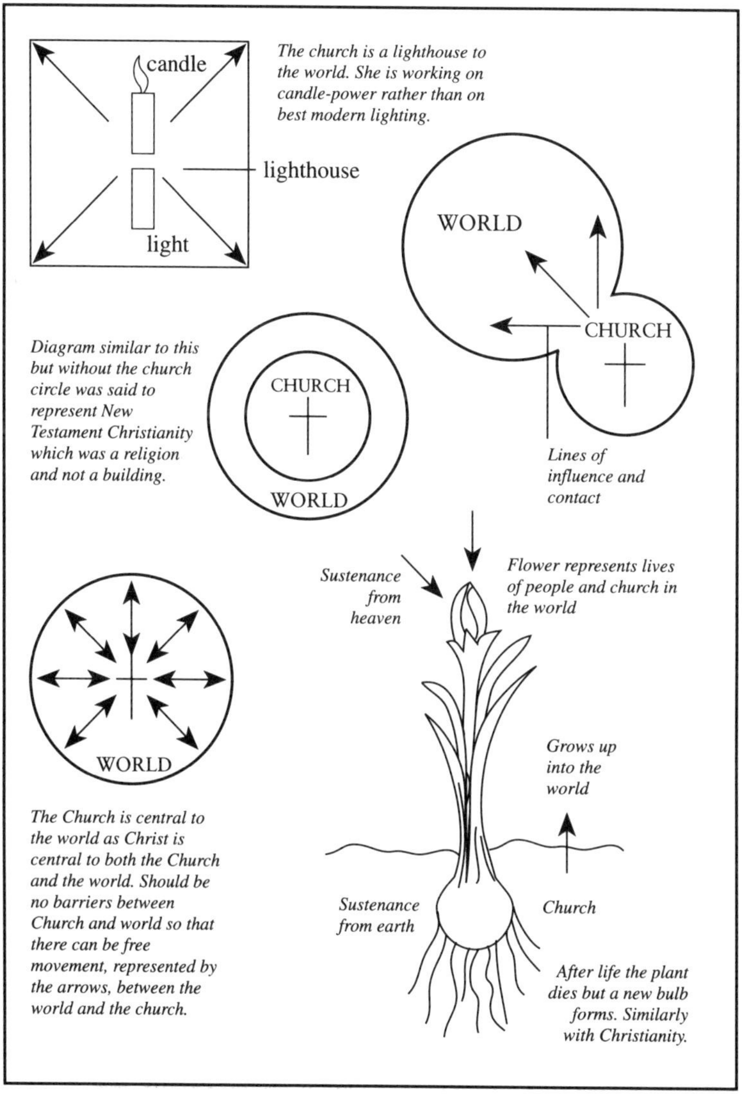


**Figure 3** A medley of mental pictures of church and world relationships

As we discussed them several things emerged. We rejected imperialistic and colonialist concepts of the church's mission to the world as we had rejected the initial model which depicted the church as using the world simply as an area from which to proselytize. Similarly we rejected any closed circle concepts of religious life. We expressed the belief that Christians are called to be in a relationship with Christ, with each other and with people in the world who are not Christians. Christ is at the centre of all these domains of human existence. Weber's idea of a 'biblical rhythm of withdrawal and return, of being the city on the mount and the salt of the earth' helped us to model this. We saw that there would be a rhythm in our lives between three domains: the church, the youth and community centre and the world at large. Figure 4 encapsulated our thinking and was subsequently widely used.

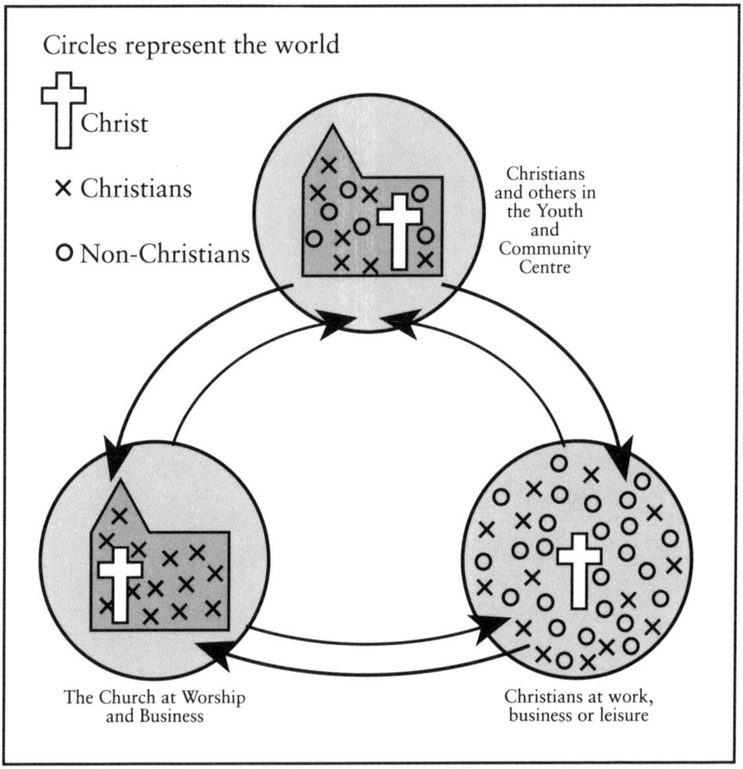


**Figure 4** Rhythm of Christian life between church, world and centre

Now we were able to see more clearly the job of promoting human and spiritual development in each of these domains and between them and that the Centre provided new opportunities to work on equal terms with people with different beliefs for interrelated development. A deeper understanding was engendered about the kind of activity appropriate to each domain and our experiences of moving between them. In the Centre it was agreed that Christian witness would be first and foremost through 'what you are, what you do and how you relate to others'. This follows the emphasis in parts of the New Testament on living the faith and being prepared to discuss it whenever it seems natural to do so or in response to questions. (cf 1 Peter 1:22; 2:9–17; 3:1–3, 8 and 15; Colossians 1:4.) Members of the conference said they needed training and support to do this.

**Spiritual life**

'Spiritual life' was an elusive and a contentious concept. As the youth and community work developed some of the Leaders and members said, 'this church is not spiritual enough', 'the spiritual life is going down', 'there is an abundance of social life but a dearth of spiritual life'. The same people would talk about the need 'to keep up our standards'. They considered themselves to be 'spiritually minded'. The criticism irritated me. I felt it was untrue and the kind of spirituality to which it referred had little attraction for me. Attempts I made to get them to define the terms and to substantiate the charge failed miserably. At one particular Leaders' Meeting I was persistent and forceful, if not a little aggressive, in my demands for definitions. Not surprisingly, some of the Leaders became hostile and aggressive towards me. I refused to define the terms for them. Some time later I saw what I was doing in a new light through reading an article by Professor Harold Garfinkel in which he describes what happened when some experimenters challenged common-sense descriptions accepted by any 'bona fide members of a collectivity'. One of the examples he quotes is this:

E *(Experimenter) waved his hand cheerily.*

S *(Subject) How are you?*

E *How am I in regard to what? My health, my finance, my school work, my peace of mind, my...*

S *(Red in the face and suddenly out of control) Look I was just trying to be polite. Frankly I don't give a damn how you are.*[4]

Garfinkel found that whenever common sense descriptions were challenged people were first perplexed and then annoyed and that those who challenge them place themselves outside the collectivity in which the common sense descriptions are used. By challenging and asking for definitions of 'spiritual life', I had placed myself outside the 'spiritual group'. Leaders reacted in the same way as those in Garfinkel's experiments. They did not believe that I, their minister, did not know what 'spiritual life' meant. Of all people, I should know what it meant; I was employed to promote spirituality!

Immediately I took a much more constructive approach to which the Leaders responded positively. They said that they were desperately concerned because they had been members of churches in which the social life and the social gospel had overshadowed the spiritual life. They believed that spiritual life was generated exclusively by worship, prayer, Bible study and Christian fellowship, not by ordinary social intercourse. A breakthrough came when I pointed out to a Leaders' Meeting that the Bible uses the word 'life' rather than 'spiritual life' to convey all that is meant to be alive to God and people. In view of this and the inability to come to agreement on the meaning of 'spiritual life', it was decided to drop the word spiritual and talk about the life of the church and the life of the centre. This caused some of those who had felt deeply 'that this church is not spiritual' to say: 'When we say that the spiritual life is going down we really mean that many people involved in Parchmore activities do not come to services of worship and this disappoints, worries and hurts us'. Others responded immediately with all the excitement of those who have just seen a mirror image point, 'There are people who regularly attend services of worship but never attend other activities. This hurts and disappoints some non-church people'. The Leaders saw, and not without some pain, that these responses to the pattern of people's participation in the various activities engenders suspicion, prejudice, hostility and hurt feelings on all sides.

One of the effects of this was a growing openness on this subject between leaders, workers and members. A majority of them had been as irritated as I had by the talk about spiritual life going down and they had felt censured and at a disadvantage because they were not considered to be 'spiritual enough' even though some of them were gracious, loving and kindly Christian people who enjoyed good relationships with people.

Now people started to understand each others positions. The pre-eminence of Christ was not disputed. There was agreement that spiritual life should be related to the whole of being. Some, however, felt that it flowed principally from God through Christ and the Church to the world whilst others believed that it flowed in all directions of human experience. The conflict derived from two quite different models of spirituality. The difference between them is represented diagrammatically in Figure 5.

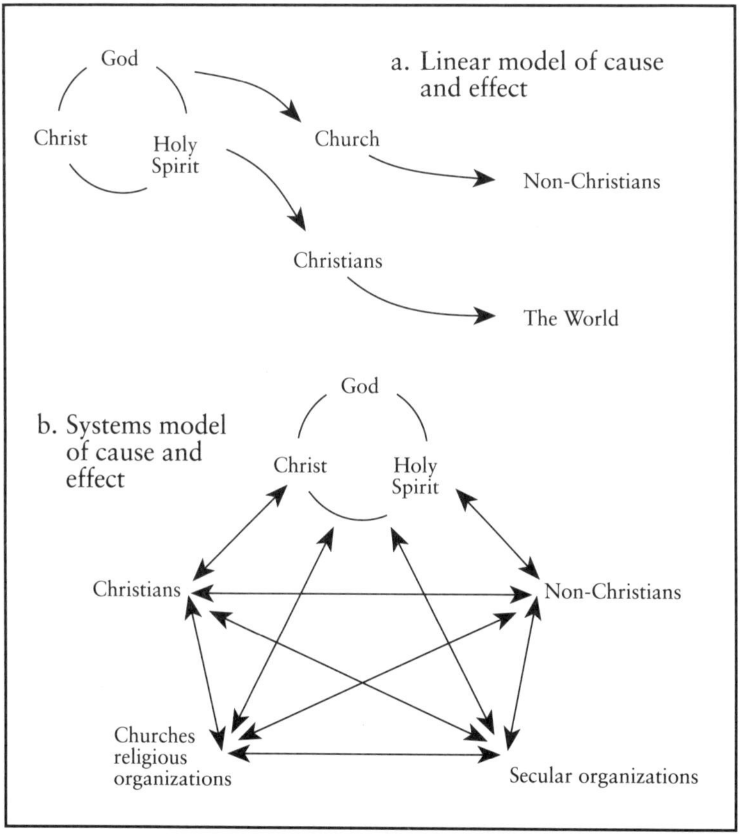


**Figure 5** Models of 'Spiritual Flow'

The first model represents a linear concept of cause and effect, the second a systemic concept in which everyone interacts with everyone else. Both models are too tidy to totally represent the two different kinds of thinking but they do represent the conceptual conflict between them. Understanding this and accepting each other's position helped us to work together, to continue a creative theological discussion and to respect a wider range of spirituality.

# — Chapter Three —
# ORIENTATION AND TRAINING

What I had learnt from the Battens' course and the consultancy sessions I had with Dr Batten throughout my ministry at Parchmore I used in my work with others in the many different ways I am describing.[1] Consequently the work that we did together was an in-service training programme for us all although we did not refer to it as such. Some things we learnt through planning work and tackling problems; other things we learnt through more formal training exercises. Both these ways of learning are illustrated in this and other chapters.

**The Parchmore workshop, September to December 1967**

Workshop sessions were held during the period September to December 1967. Aims for the project were defined (cf pp22f). Then members worked in a group on one of the following aspects of community work: play/group facilities; retired peoples' needs; ex-mental health patients in need of rehabilitation in the community; a counselling service; a homework club for children from overcrowded homes. Significant programmes of work eventually evolved on the first four of these areas. The fifth was a failure because we provided something for young people on what we thought was their need. All arrangements were made. I visited schools. We waited. No young people came. It is not possible here to describe the playgroup which quickly became a thriving over-subscribed five day a week organization with a life of its own. A part-time community worker, Mrs Rebecca Brown, was appointed to work with the mothers of the children in the playgroup. Nor is it possible to describe the counselling service. The other two are discussed.

Some people found it very difficult to know which group to join because they were equally interested in several subjects. During the first group-work session they remained undecided. Immediately after the meeting a considerable number of people moved forward and surrounded me at the blackboard. They were in an animated condition not normal for middle-class church people. With considerable emotion they demanded that I tell them which group they should join. They shouted at me in some anger, 'You know what you want us to do and what we should do. Tell us instead of going on and on like this'. As courteously as I could I declined to tell them what they ought to do. Eventually I fixed my attention on one person and shouted to be heard above the clamour, 'Do you know what you want to do?' 'No!' came the angry answer. 'How on earth can I know then?!', I replied. The point was taken. Then as best I was able under the circumstances I explained to the group that I did not know, and could not know, what they ought to do when they did not know. I also explained that what I was doing was an attempt to help them to decide what to do and to say why they should do it. When they had calmed down, one person said, and the others agreed, 'A fortnight is too long to wait to take up the subject, we should be meeting in the morning'. Most people came to the next session prepared and determined to make decisions. They did not ask me to tell them what to do again but they did ask me to help them to decide what to do.

When I told Dr Batten about this incident expecting sympathy he said, 'Good. You are really getting somewhere now!'

This was a critical point in the establishment of my role as a non-directive group worker. From their experience over many years they expected their minister to tell them what to do. I was acting non-traditionally and all of us found it difficult.

Another highly significant feature of the workshop occurred during the last of the six sessions we had planned when careful consideration was given to the future of the workshop. After much intensive discussion the members concluded that:

- the workshop ought not to meet again: (This would help the groups to become autonomous, to recruit new members and to get on with their work at their own pace.)
- groups should appoint 'workers'. ('Groups function most efficiently', they said, 'when they have someone to help structure their thinking and discussion, not in an authoritarian directive way but non-directively, from a neutral point of view.')
- group leaders should liaise; in two or three months time there should be a consultation representative of all the groups who use, or who are going to use the Centre.

The decision to end the workshop was difficult to make. All the sessions had been well-attended and people had found them interesting. The natural inclination of Methodists once they have organized a successful series of meetings is 'to keep it going'. Had this decision not been taken future developments could have been frustrated because people would have had to put time and energy into maintaining the workshop meetings rather than getting on with the work.

**Other formal training**

One of the results of this continuous use of the non-directive approach was that people asked for more formal training. For instance, after I had been using it for two years the members of the 1969 Sunbury Conference, the second of three residential conferences during my ministry, asked me to demonstrate it because, they said, 'It enables successful and fruitful discussion. It is a most important subject because so many developments in our community life are set in motion by groups of people thinking and planning together.' So, there and then, I led a group of six volunteers on 'the "how" of communication', a subject they chose whilst some seventy people observed. Then we examined what had happened. This was a profound learning experience about the functions of a non-directive worker and group dynamics.

Developing the comprehensive Christian education and training programme (cf pp43ff) involved formal training sessions on biblical and theological subjects, on teaching methods and on group work. Initially I led these sessions although others made inputs but after a year or so the teachers themselves conducted them and I had monthly work consultancy sessions with the superintendent similar to the ones I had with Dr Batten (see below).

Some leaders and workers from the youth centre went on local authority and Methodist training courses.

Some four years after I had been at Parchmore different individuals and groups representative of the diverse aspects of the church, youth and community work asked me for 'a plain statement of the ideas behind the working methods we practise at Parchmore'. Arrangements were made for me to make such a statement at the 1971 Teach In. Drawing heavily upon a book I was writing[(2)] I described the basic ideas about community development, about working with people for the interrelated development of church and community and about directive and non-directive approaches and how I saw these things expressing

Christian beliefs. Christians and non-Christians attended the lecture, discussed it vigorously for a long time afterwards. A record of the lecture and the discussion produced by the late Dorothy Household was widely circulated and studied.[3]

The productivity of these formal training sessions was out of all proportion to the short amount of time given to them. This I attribute to the way in which they grew out of and drew upon a long intensive period of common experience of putting the approach into practice.

People of all ages were involved in all of this. For some it was a learning experience which proceeded in parallel with formative years in their school and vocational education from, say, thirteen to nineteen years of age or sixteen to twenty-two. For others of us it was a programme of adult education by which we were re-formed and re-trained for church and community work.

**Consultancy help**

My training continued after I had completed the Battens' course, because Dr Batten offered to discuss with me problems or plans in relation to my work at Parchmore on an ad hoc basis. I gladly took up the offer and a consultancy relationship was soon firmly established. He also offered to supervise my further studies in relation to the Parchmore work which eventually led to my doctorate.

Dr Batten was consultant to me, not consultant to Parchmore as one of the Ten Centres, nor to the Parchmore people. This was a valuable continuation of the course by which again Parchmore got Dr Batten's help through me. This was possible because as Dr Batten himself worked non-directively, I never felt that he was imposing ideas or a special line of action upon me nor, through me, upon the people. Thus we, the local people and I, remained responsible for the work and I always felt we were free to decide what we wished to do. What Dr Batten did was to help me to conceptualize situations and problems more clearly, to draw my attention to possible courses of action that I had not thought of, to stimulate and help me weight up the pros and cons of each alternative more thoroughly and to help me to see ways of working *with* rather than *for* people.

The consultations were arranged at my request about subjects, plans or problems on which I had decided I wanted consultancy help. Consequently the starting point of each consultation was an issue I raised, normally verbally, at the beginning of the consultation. The consultations were most helpful because Dr Batten had the facility to conceptualize the issues quickly and accurately and because I always felt that he had grasped the situation in which I found myself. Also he helped me to control my emotional involvement and to take it into account in evaluating my observations. Consultations generally lasted three hours. Dr Batten made himself available when needed. This was an extremely important factor, for it meant that every interview dealt with live issues. At one time and another almost every aspect of the project was discussed. The interest of the Battens in me and my work and their support was of inestimable value.

## — Chapter Four —
## DESIGNING AND PLANNING

Much was learnt in Parchmore about the important art of designing development work programmes with people. This section gives some examples.

**Retired people and their needs**

The workshop group (cf p31) on the needs of people in the church and neighbourhood who were retired had about fifteen members and had seven meetings in addition to those held during the workshop.

At their February 1968 meeting, which was the first I had attended, the group members listed the amenities for retired people in the area around Parchmore. This was followed by unsuccessful attempts to identify unmet needs. After this discussion had proceeded for some time I made the observation that the only people not contributing to the discussion were those who were retired. (Later I discovered that this had happened in the workshop. It indicates just how deeply ingrained is the 'doing for' approach. The retired were passive; the non-retired active. A debilitating collusion. A variation on 'Does she take sugar?') This remark caused one member to blurt out immediately, 'We should be asking them (the retired people) what they want, instead of saying what we think they want. How ridiculous! Here we've been talking about what retired people want and haven't had the sense to ask those sitting next to us.' The retired people made a few suggestions but then they said, 'But we're church people. What we need to know is what other people in the community want'. Again, breaking out of yet another 'doing for' trap.

By now the group was thinking intensively. There was an air of expectation and excitement about the meeting. Members were trying to find ways of getting to know from retired people themselves what their needs were. It was agreed that they would be most likely to share this in the security of their own homes as they chatted over a cup of tea with a trusted friend. The group said the best thing to do was to select twenty roads round Parchmore and find someone to visit one old person known to them in that road. I asked whether the visitors would need any information and how the replies would be recorded. The members of the group said they needed something to guide them through the discussions, a statement and questions. They would use them either to ask the questions and fill in the questionnaire on the spot or just ask the questions and then fill in the questionnaire afterwards. Two retired people took the lead. The group moved to sit round a table and the two people drafted the suggestions, the edited version they produced later is given in Display 2.

> On behalf of a small group of people in the Parchmore Youth and Community Centre we are trying to find out whether the new centre can be used during the daytime for activities which would meet some of the needs of retired people.
>
> Would you be interested in:
>
> ☐ A morning Coffee Club where you could play table games and read the papers in a warm modern centre?
>
> ☐ A luncheon Club?
>
> ☐ A hobbies and Handicrafts Club?
>
> Which Hobbies/Handicrafts? ______________________
>
> ______________________
>
> Have you any other suggestions to make? ______________________
>
> ______________________
>
> Would you be interested in:
>
> ☐ Men only group ☐ Women only group ☐ Mixed group
>
> What time of day would suit you best? ______________________
>
> Would you like to be notified of any developments? ☐ yes ☐ no
>
> Name ______________________
>
> Address ______________________
>
> ______________________
>
> *We must point out that this information is wanted for our guidance and we cannot promise what will be provided at this stage.*

**Display 2** Retired peoples' questionnaire

The group met in March 1968 to make arrangements for the visits to be made. In May and June they met to consider the twenty-eight questionnaires which had been completed. The most popular need was for a Thursday morning coffee club and the next most popular for a luncheon club. It was decided to start a coffee club and to allow this to develop into a coffee and luncheon club if requested by the retired people. By now the retired people in the group were taking a lead and doing most of the work.

A coffee club was started in October 1968. In February 1969, a year after my first meeting with the group, we met to review the developments in the club. It had an average attendance of twenty-five and had money in hand from the sale of coffee. I asked the group members who they considered should have responsibility for the club. They decided 'that the club members should have as much say in their own affairs as they are prepared to have'. It was suggested that I should meet with the members of the club in the summer to ask them to consider whether they wished to take over responsibility for their club and become more and more self-programming. The group considered that they would have made their contribution if the retired people accepted responsibility for the club and, therefore, agreed that the group would be disbanded if the club became autonomous. All the members of the group said they would be prepared to help in any way they could.

In July 1969 I met the club members. They were sitting in small groups around card tables drinking coffee. These proved to be useful 'buzz' groups. I reminded them how the club had come into existence and that the original group had suggested they be asked if they wished to take charge of their club. I explained what this might mean. After each statement or question I allowed time for them to talk to each other in their 'table groups'. A typical conversation went something like this.

*First person: What did he say, could you hear him?*

*Second person: Who is he anyway?*

*Third person: The Vicar. Do we want to run the club for ourselves.*

*Fourth person: What does he mean? What will we have to do?*

*Second person: Vote on this and that I suppose and decide on outings and subs and things.*

*Fourth person: He said we could have charge of our own money too, if we want, that is.*

*Fifth person: He's the minister not the vicar.*

*First person: Think it's a good idea?*

*Third person: I'm not sure. It's all right as it is.*

*Second person: But it would be our club then.*

*Third person: Yes, it would...*

Eventually, after a lot of such discussion they agreed to accept responsibility and there and then elected officers.

The club grew gradually and the members slowly took more and more responsibility for it. By 1972 it was well-established as a self-directing club with an average attendance of thirty and a club life which suited its members. By 1977 I understand it was a thriving club with an average attendance of forty. Then it played a key role in developing and staffing two one-day a week self-directing luncheon clubs, one for retired people and another for retired people who were handicapped. It also played a key role in establishing a local good neighbour scheme through which retired people, in co-operation with various agencies, 'cover' all elderly people in their neighbourhood who are at risk. Most of those organizing this scheme were retired. A statutory social worker said that the scheme would never have 'got off the ground' without the experience gained by setting up and running a self-determining coffee club. In addition, all this work played an important part in Parchmore securing the appointment of a full-time community worker. All this underlines the importance of slow beginnings and gradual growth.

**Rehabilitation of ex-mental health patients**

Parchmore became one of the Ten Centres at a time when the Croydon Association for Mental Health was founded. Over a period of a year before, during and after the workshop there was much discussion between members of this vigorous association and some Parchmore people about basing a 'rehabilitation and care club' at Parchmore. Parchmore's contribution would be providing premises and refreshments. Professional people would do the social and community work. There were endless discussions and considerable pressure to start a club immediately. A club was not started because whilst we were keen to make a contribution we did not want to see Parchmore premises rented for other people to do community work. We wished to be involved in any activities we promoted in an 'informed and responsible way' and in 'equal partnership' with other people or agencies. And we felt that it would be better to spend a year preparing 'to do a real job' than to start immediately in 'an amateurish way'.

During the workshop sessions the information that had been obtained and the ideas which had been worked out were introduced into the discussions by people who had been involved in the exploratory work. A new group was formed to investigate further what Parchmore could contribute towards the rehabilitation of ex-mental health patients. This group recruited a person with experience in mental health from another organization to act as their group worker. After seeking further information and advice about what was happening in the field of mental health members of the group decided that it was not advisable to organize such a club at Parchmore. They thought a more important contribution could be made towards the 'integration of people into the community' through existing Parchmore organizations. Examining this possibility and making the necessary arrangements was something they felt they could do.

The group decided they needed to consider: How can ex-mental health patients who live in the locality be 'discovered'? How, in co-operation with the psychiatric social workers, should they be approached? How should they be introduced to Parchmore organizations and activities? Pursuing these questions led the group to realize that the success of its plans depended upon having sympathetic contacts in Parchmore organizations and effective liaison with people in the mental welfare department. Therefore, they decided to convene a meeting of their group with the psychiatric social workers, representatives of the Parchmore organizations they thought could contribute to the rehabilitation of people in normal community life (drama, wives, community and youth clubs, women's and men's fellowships and the Counselling Group) and with the youth worker and me. They circulated a statement of what they were trying to do along with the invitation to the meeting.

The meeting was held in April 1968. Twenty-two people attended including two psychiatric social workers. By invitation I acted as worker to the group. This was an extraordinary meeting where people shared their feelings and thoughts openly and at depth. There were two areas of concern which people worked through before they turned to discussing the scheme.

The first concern was that of their fears of the patients. They said that 'we are scared to invite them to come and maybe they are scared to come'. They thought this fear resulted from ignorance and was generated when people were labelled 'ex-mental health patients'. Whilst education about mental health might reduce this fear they thought the most practical way for Parchmore people to deal with it was for them to get to know ex-mental health patients as people. The second concern was about meeting ex-mental health patients and introducing them to Parchmore organizations. People were worried that this might involve them in having to neglect their friends and spend all their time looking after ex-patients. They discussed this topic for a long time. The psychiatric social workers helped people to see that they would be required to be friends and not amateur psychiatrists to the patients. I asked them if there were any other experiences which would help them in thinking about this subject. Eventually they fixed upon their experiences of welcoming and introducing new people at work. They went through this stage by stage drawing upon their experiences. They said how important it was to have someone who was friendly and interested and sympathetic, who introduced you to people and gave you information and tips when you went to a new job. They said how the newcomers eventually found their own way round and made their own friends. And, whilst a special relationship always existed between befrienders and the newcomers, the latter gradually became less dependent on the befrienders. ('He/she doesn't cling as much!')

Having settled these issues to their satisfaction they turned to the task of working out the best way to organize the scheme. During this part of the session I constructed diagrams showing the inter-personal relationships being discussed and wrote out statements to clarify what was being said. The points made were:

- Psychiatric social workers and psychiatrists who know the needs of the patients should prescribe which organization is most likely to help them in the same way that doctors prescribe medicines, treatments and convalescence. To do this successfully they will need information about Parchmore organizations.

- The psychiatric social workers should advise Parchmore people on the best way in which to meet and introduce patients to an organization or activity because each patient is different and has different needs. For example, it may be absolutely essential for one patient's recovery that he/she makes his/her own way to a new organization whereas another would have to be escorted.
- The success of this scheme will depend upon the ratio between 'patients' and 'non-patients' in any one organization being similar to that which exists in the community. If the membership of an organization contains a high number of patients it would not have the same therapeutic value for the patients. Local people would refer to organizations or Parchmore in a derogatory way as 'the loony bin'. (These were arguments against a rehabilitation and care club.) Other members might not find their needs satisfied, and leave.

They felt that because of my pastoral and counselling work, my co-ordinating role in Parchmore, and my place on the Executive of the Croydon Association for Mental Health that I should act as a liaison member between the mental health professional worker, and statutory and voluntary agencies and the organizations.

The organizations considered by the psychiatric social workers most useful in this work were Axis, a community club for people of all ages, the youth club and the wives' club. These organizations were willing to participate in the project.

It was essential to confirm that the organizations were agreeable to the scheme as it had now been worked out before it was put into operation.

This became known as the 'Parchmore Rehabilitation Model'.

The scheme was put into operation almost immediately. One of the psychiatric social workers spent a considerable amount of time visiting and appraising the organizations at Parchmore in order to help him to decide who would benefit from joining them. Two or three people were introduced to the youth centre and the wives' club but they did not stay very long. During 1968-69, however, no less than seven people were introduced to Axis under this scheme.

Two did not settle, one attended spasmodically for a year, another regularly for about two years and in 1972 three had been attending for five years and were integrated members of the club. The psychiatric social worker responsible for the introduction of two of the latter was amazed they stayed so long and the changes it had brought about in their lives. The third was stabilized considerably. Modest but significant contributions.

**The inauguration of a comprehensive Christian education programme, October 1968**

A momentous step was taken when a comprehensive programme of education was inaugurated in October 1968. It brought together six organizations with quite different theological emphases and educational expertise which up to this point had contributed separately to the Christian education of young people in Parchmore: the Sunday School, the Boys' Brigade, Guides and Brownies, the Junior Missionary Association, The Morning Star. What emerged was a new organization for education set out in this way:

- From October 1968 a comprehensive educational programme should be in operation at Parchmore designed as an integral part of the morning worshipping community and to help make worship more meaningful to the whole church.
- This programme should be based on the British Lesson Council's new syllabus which adopted the experiential approach to Christian education. Teachers should be appointed to departments but not to classes. It was thought that this would increase flexibility by enabling the departments to arrange different groups for different teaching situations.
- All teachers should attend a monthly in-service training and preparation class which I should lead on Sunday afternoons.
- The 'school' should be held from 10.30 to 11.30am on each Sunday in the month apart from Community Worship Services (see the next point) the members and staff of the school would be in church for 'a hymn, a prayer and a Bible reading', and would then proceed immediately to their departments. At 11.30am coffee and soft drinks would be served in the Centre for the members of the school and the congregation.

- A service of community worship should be held each month. The uniformed organizations should parade to these services. The content of the services would be related to what was being taught in the departments.
- The Sunday School Council should be replaced by a Christian Education Council on which all those engaged in the formal education of children and young people would be represented.
- A superintendent should be appointed for Christian Education who should meet monthly for consultations with the minister about the Christian education programme.

Later it was decided to call the whole of the morning assembly: 'Ten Thirty Church'.

There were many positive results of implementing this programme. There was a considerable increase in the number of children and young people participating in formal Christian education and a great improvement in the regularity with which they attended. Indeed by 1971/72 the young people's department had become so large that accommodation was only just adequate. New staff members were recruited from another church in the Circuit to deal with the influx. Bringing together young people from different organizations formally in educational groups and informally in the coffee bar after Ten Thirty Church helped to form several new friendship groups and networks. Young people participated in a far wider range of activities. Community worship became more and more popular with people of all age groups and made important contributions to their education. Worship and education in the church were much more integrated than they had ever been. People realized that the community development approaches were relevant to working out things to do with education and worship.

Making these changes, however, was a very tricky business requiring a lot of care and patience. Pressure of any kind would have wrecked the negotiations. Of the many things which contributed to the good outcome I mention a few. Everyone involved contributed freely. It had not always been so. An incident during the early days of my ministry at Parchmore illustrates the change and how it came about. The teachers and I were spending a lot of time trying to save and rebuild the Sunday School. On one occasion in the midst of our analysis of the situation one of the teachers, a housewife with no special training in education, made a contribution. She was so nervous that she was at times inarticulate. There was some embarrassment in the group because her thinking did not fit the thought patterns we were following. Her intervention was in danger of being ignored and she was in danger of being frozen out, howbeit quite politely. Instinctively I felt that there was something very profound about what she was saying and I encouraged and helped her to explain and develop her thinking. The ideas she contributed that night greatly helped us to redeem the situation. Two years later I discovered that that was the first time she had spoken out at those meetings which she had been attending for thirteen years! Amongst other things this freedom meant that everyone expressed quite openly any niggles and fears that they had. In fact we came to an understanding quite early in the discussions that we would work through any and all difficulties or fears until we felt they had been dealt with. To gloss or avoid them, we agreed, would lead to plans unlikely to work. So we stayed with this and that worry. At times it was not easy to do so because people were inclined to become impatient when worries which were not theirs were 'holding us up' and there didn't seem any way of overcoming them. But we did work at things together until we all felt we could go on. Mutual caring grew and as it did working relationships deepened and helped us to weather crises. All this is illustrated by one of the crises.

After months of negotiations the Boys' Brigade Officers felt they simply had to withdraw from the discussions. This was a traumatic time for us all. Several things brought them to this position. They were worried that the boys in the Brigade would react negatively to what they would see as 'joining the Sunday School' ('a soppy activity') and mixing with girls and children. They feared they would react in this way even if a new name and time was found for the educational programme. Another worry was to do with the kind of educational programme envisaged. Officers and boys were used to a formal didactic approach to the Bible class which was modelled on a service of worship. The officers were good at this but they felt threatened and de-skilled by the sophisticated educational methods used by the Sunday School teachers. They doubted their ability to teach in this way and, even if they could, they felt the boys would prefer the Bible class approach. One of the things that helped us to work through this crisis was that a Boys'

Brigade national commission had recently recommended the introduction of experiential education and co-operation with local churches on Christian education programmes.[1] The Boys' Brigade nationally had sought my help in working out the implications of these recommendations and the Parchmore officers were pleased about this. So there was stimulus from within and the kudos gained by following up the Brigade's new thinking. However, possibly the thing that helped most, was that their feelings were treated with deep understanding and great respect. There was no recrimination. On the contrary others responded by speaking about their fears more openly. The officers were given time to work through their feelings. Eventually they felt they could continue when it was agreed that any arrangements should be carefully monitored, that snags should be sorted out as soon as they were identified, that there should be a trial period and when contingency plans were made to cover the possibility that the programme failed to work. This understanding and long-standing associations between some of the teachers, the Boys' Brigade and the officers helped to work through the crisis. In fact the officers became pillars of the new programme and rejoiced in the new methods.

**The inauguration of the Parchmore Church Youth and Community Council**

The Parchmore Church Youth and Community Council was inaugurated in May 1970 after two-and-a half years searching for an organizational pattern which would more readily facilitate people from all the organizations working with each other in organizing and administering and developing the work. It transformed the organization and power structures of Parchmore.

A community meeting in January 1969 defined the organizational difficulties that had to be overcome as follows:

- There are too many meetings and committees.
- Difficulties of communication between groups are increasing.
- The time taken in getting the opinions of committees on practical and policy matters can be prolonged and this severely hampers progress.

- The self-programming groups which have developed from the workshop 'have not got access to the governing bodies of the church'.
- There is an organizational division between 'religious' and 'social' work.
- It is difficult for church and non-church people to work together as equals because only members of the Methodist Church can vote in meetings that control policy.
- Leaders, Trust and Youth Council Meetings spend little time discussing policy.
- The minister is the only ex officio member of all committees and therefore co-ordination of the work largely depends upon him.
- The standard Methodist organization is inadequate for a church, youth and community centre.

Redesigning the organizations structure to overcome these problems was fascinating but difficult. Amongst other things we all learned about the approach we were adopting. During one of the meetings I asked if there were any suggestions for solving the problems other than the ideas already expressed at previous meetings. One of the Leaders said he had an idea and got out an excellent visual aid to illustrate it which he had hidden at the back of the room. I had no knowledge of this suggestion before this moment. The Leader who made the suggestion was the husband of the secretary of the meeting who was seated next to me. Whilst her husband was organizing his visual aid, she lent over and pointed to a page of notes which I was using during the meeting and said words to the effect that this foiled my plans. She had always thought that I used the non-directive method to introduce my own ideas in such a way that the people thought that they had suggested them. She thought that I stimulated people to make suggestions until the one I had in mind was mentioned and then settled on that one and excluded the others. I asked her to read my notes. She was utterly amazed and confounded to find that they consisted of a resume of what had happened in previous discussions, alternative ways of proceeding with the business, a possible order of business (which had been reversed in the first few minutes of the meeting by the Leaders) and questions which had to be dealt with by the meeting in regard to any other proposed solutions. Subsequently neither she, nor any other Leaders, accused me of 'fishing' for the suggestion I wished to support. It was a moment of revelation and conviction about the integrity of my use of the non-directive approach.

Several people produced ideas. The one I produced did not gain much favour. The one that did was proposed by an elderly man. Everyone in the meeting got hold of it long before I did. I simply could not see what he meant. The Leaders helped me to do so. This idea formed the basis of a Council representative of all the organizations related to Parchmore which overcame or minimized the difficulties. The categories of membership and their duties were laid out as were the functions of the Council. As the Constitutional Practice and Discipline of the Methodist Church did not permit such an arrangement we had to seek permission from above. We got that and in fact the legislation was altered to take account of the difficulties we had experienced.

Up to the time that I left, the Council met ten times with an average attendance of twenty-three. Quite quickly the members got it working well on a medley of things to do with the everyday life of the Centre such as timetabling, use of premises and equipment, dealing with mice and using blackouts. Alongside these subjects they started to accept some joint responsibility for fund-raising. They were consulted about my successor. Never before had the church members been consulted about the appointment of a minister. Now members and non-members representative of church and community were consulted. At their first meeting they were asked to organize a teach in about Parchmore and the methods being used, and they did (cf p33). They set up working parties to deal with faction over allocation of premises. For my part I encouraged them to work on policy and took to them any matters that I could. When I had to act between meetings on anything upon which they had not determined policy, I reported to them what I had done and asked them to decide about future policy in relation to similar eventualities.

The Council became a community forum. It performed some of the problem solving functions which it was hoped that it would. It built up new lines of communication and understanding between the various organizations. The number of meetings necessary to run the church and Centre was considerably reduced. A sequence of principal committee and council meetings was worked out which enabled matters to be processed from committee to committee with minimum delay.

There was a general feeling of relief and satisfaction that we had tackled and solved to our satisfaction considerable organizational difficulties.

# — Chapter Five —
# PROBLEM SOLVING

We always seemed to be tackling problems of one kind or another. Sometimes we were working together harmoniously to overcome difficulties. There are four examples of this kind of activity in the previous chapter related to retired people, ex-mental health patients, Christian education and a community council. At other times the problems were associated with people falling out with each other and heated arguments over such things as the use of crockery and rooms. Then there were problems generated by aggression and violence which led to the breakdown of relationships and organizations. Three questions helped us to work at difficulties together and to tackle problems. They were:

- What is the problem? (Definition)
- Why does it occur? (Diagnosis)
- What can we do about it? (Action)[1]

Completing the sequence from definition through diagnosis to action (or to a conscious decision not to act) meant we were working at problems not simply talking about them. We used another approach alongside this one. It involved groups of leaders building up pictures of what was happening in clubs, organizations and the church by observing events carefully, searching for explanations of what they had seen and then deciding what action to take. This was a thorough-going way of learning from experience through a do-it-yourself form of action research: that is a way of gathering and piecing together the information that people have of their working situations so that they can understand them better and take effective action. In this chapter there are examples of using both these methods in tackling the problems encountered.

**Premises, crockery cupboards and the stage**
Allocating the new premises was approached apprehensively. There were conflicting demands. Traditionally, accommodation and storage were allocated by the Stewards and the Trustees. Making arrangements in this way had often led to trouble and faction. Long before the new premises were completed

organizations were lobbying and using their influence to get the rooms they wanted when they wanted them and to get a good share of the best storage space.

The members of the workshop considered these problems and suggested a consultation representative of the people who were going to use the new premises before they were opened. I reported this to the Trustees and got them to look at the pros and cons of different ways of allocating the new premises. They agreed to a consultative procedure being adopted and said they would not veto any suggestions agreeable to the Chapel Stewards and the members of the meeting. This was an unprecedented procedure in Parchmore.

A meeting was convened of representatives of all the organizations who would be using the premises to allocate the accommodation and storage. It was well attended, organizations had sent those most capable of looking after their interests. Representatives were asked to consult their organizations about their needs before coming to the meeting. The Senior Chapel Stewards and I decided that the best way to deal with all the complications of allocating so many premises to so many organizations was to prepare a wall chart to be completed at the meeting. The chart had a horizontal band marked off for the days of the week and the hours of the day for each part of the premises. This enabled everyone to identify the problems of trying to fit everything in and to suggest solutions. The Stewards prepared the chart and filled it in at the meeting whilst I helped the members of the meeting to discuss and decide. People who under the traditional system of allocating premises were belligerent about their territorial rights worked willingly to ensure that as many of the needs of all the organizations as possible were met in the best way. Before the meeting closed, people said how successful the meeting had been; that people were more willing to give and take in this than in former situations; that the task had been accomplished quickly; and that they ought to meet again in this way to discuss other common concerns and particularly the vexed question of cutlery, crockery and kitchen utensils. Tackling this concern introduced people to the problem solving sequence described above which they came to value.

Friction and unpleasant arguments between individuals and organizations were associated with cutlery, crockery and kitchen utensils. Each organization had its own locked cupboard.

Sometimes crockery was left out unwashed. Those who used the premises next had to clean up the mess left by others. People got annoyed about this. Sometimes they washed the crockery and locked it in their own cupboards. Crockery cupboards were broken into. Additional locks were fitted. Some had as many as three locks, to prevent doors being prised open. The situation was out of hand. Feelings were running strong. Everyone was exasperated and many were feeling guilty because they thought this sort of thing should not happen in a Christian organization: it was a denial of all we believed about sharing; the cupboards took up valuable space and got in the way; there was more crockery than was needed. The Stewards responsible for such things and I organized a meeting of representatives of all the organizations with crockery cupboards, twenty-five people or so. We used the three questions and kept people to them: What is the problem? Why does it occur? What are we going to do about it? Accusation, counter-accusation and argument gradually gave way to rational exchanges and bargaining. We actually worked out a way of having a common stock of crockery and the ground rules by which such a scheme could work. Much of the detail of the arrangements I have long forgotten but one thing I will never forget. All at once the members of the meeting realized that they had got a result, they had reached an amicable solution and that warm and generous feelings now pervaded. There was a lovely silence for a moment or two and then a man stood up and said, 'Well, if we can solve that one we can solve anything. What is next on the agenda?' Laughter of agreement and consent rippled through the group.

Some time later there was an enormous row about the use of the stage. Facing up to this problem was an important learning situation about 'spiritual life'. The Drama Club was rehearsing a play and the Wives' Club a concert. Both organizations put on productions of a high standard. Other organizations used the large hall which contained the stage. Practices overran their practice time and caused considerable difficulties for the uniformed organizations. Again we called a meeting of representatives of the organizations involved and got into the now familiar routine What is the problem? Why does it occur? What can we do about it? At first there were a lot of angry exchanges. Gradually as the emotion spent itself we worked at the actualities through a large chart which set out just when and how the hall and the stage were used. This showed that the pressure was on the evenings because that was the only time when some people were free. No one would give way. For some time there was an impasse with renewed recriminations. Then the representative of the Wives' Club made a reconciling move. Her organization had prior rights on the use of the stage at prime times. She saw the possibility of meeting during the day to rehearse some items. She offered to give up some of the evening time. The fighting stopped. Members of the meeting started to work together and found mutually acceptable solutions. The person who had started the row through losing his temper was a devout Christian committed to the idea of spiritual life flowing through the Church and Christians to the world (cf p29). The person who started the process of reconciliation was not a Christian. This profoundly affected the group and the person who had started the row. He apologized and acknowledged that he had learnt an important 'Christian' lesson from a non-Christian about the way in which grace can flow from non-Christians to Christians. Subsequently he quoted this incident in many contexts as an example of the way in which people outside the church can promote development within it. It caused him to move away from a simple and towards a comprehensive way of thinking about the flow of grace (cf p29).

The way in which these things were done had a profound effect on later developments. The people used what they had learned from such experiences to solve other problems. When they were compelled to devise a more adequate organizational structure they used the consultative method they first experienced in allocating the premises. (cf pp46ff and p50ff)

**Aggressive behaviour in the youth centre: the November crisis, 1968**

Early in my ministry a group of twelve young people closely associated with the church asked me if it was possible for them to have a Saturday night youth club. Permission was given by the church. Leaders were eventually found. Young people and leaders together organized a club and ran it successfully, first on Saturday evenings and then on Saturday and Tuesday evenings. Previous clubs had been ruined by the destructive behaviour of an influx of non-members. To avoid this they controlled entry and membership. By and large this worked although there were crises from time to time when groups of youths tried to force an entry.

These clubs, started in October 1966, took their place as going concerns in the Youth Centre when it opened in May 1968.

Over the same period an enormous amount of effort had gone into making arrangements for the open youth work in the new Centre. A new management committee had been formed. Miss Penny Thatcher a full-time youth worker had been appointed and voluntary workers and helpers recruited. There were, however, unresolved differences of opinion between them about the number of people who ought to be allowed to join the Centre and the terms of membership. Some said that as it was an open centre anyone should be allowed to attend at any time. For them the thought of large numbers of people in the Centre spelt success. Others said that to open the doors to anyone at any time was irresponsible. They wished to see the kind of steady and controlled growth which had occurred in the Saturday and Tuesday Clubs.

On the night of the opening of the Centre over a hundred and twenty young people attended. Thereafter the Centre was open on three evenings a week. During the first week the three hundred limit was reached, the membership list closed and two hundred young people were turned away and a 'members only' policy was introduced. This was not adhered to rigidly. Anyone could open locked doors to let people in. Even helpers were doing this and when one was challenged about her actions she said, 'I just can't say no. They begged to come in and they promised they wouldn't cause any trouble'. Other helpers felt the same way.

However, there was a good atmosphere in the Centre during the first few months. The youth worker and some of the leaders and helpers had already established good relationships with about one hundred of the members. People were very pleased that it was so popular, not least because it vindicated all that they had done to meet what they considered to be a real need. They were also pleased to see that about a third of those using the Centre were West Indians. The leaders and helpers found the developments exciting and they were full of hope for the future although they did not know how to deal with so many new people all at once.

Both leaders and helpers were recruited locally from churches and the community. All the leaders received their basic training through the LEA courses. Some leaders had started as helpers in the Centre and graduated to leaders when they had completed their training courses. In order that we might learn together how to do the work in which we were engaged we organized from September 1968 monthly 'Youth Club Helpers' Meetings'. Much of the formal in-service training of all the adults working in the Centre was effected through these meetings to which I acted as group worker. We dealt with practical matters but most of the time was given to rigorous study of the theory and practice of the work in which we were engaged. The meetings were grand learning experiences.

In spite of all this we found ourselves unable to deal with the influx of new members and to establish relationships with some of them. These young people frustrated attempts made by adults to enter into conversation with them either by ignoring them completely, abusing them with foul language or by trying to make fun of them. Gradually more and more damage was done to the building and the equipment. Billiard balls were thrown around. During this period coffee tables were inverted and used in a frightening game of 'bumper cars', toilet cisterns and other fittings were ripped from the walls and the premises flooded, obscene words and suggestions were painted on walls, windows were broken, money stolen, members climbed all over the building, threw fireworks into the Centre and into rooms where other groups were meeting. The police were called in by the neighbours and, on one or two occasions, reluctantly, by the leaders. Up to October 1968 the violence was in the main against property rather than people, but it then turned to people. Members started to catapult pointed steel staples at other members and helpers and there were fights. Some were armed with dangerous knives and other weapons. By November 1968 the situation was critical.

Euphoria had turned to unhappiness, the hope to disillusionment and the excitement to worry and fear. The Centre was wrecked by 'skinheads', people were hurt, police had to be called, the Centre had to be closed. Some people said that they had told 'us' that this would happen. They had, and the 'expert' who was trying to persuade Parchmore to become a centre said that 'professional' youth workers now knew how to deal with such problems.

Facing up to these problems involved me in discussions with neighbours (they were irate), church leaders and members (they were variously disillusioned, angry and hurt) and youth workers in the Centre, I was acting as a mediator between them. Two basic kinds of response were made. The one is epitomized in sayings such as: 'Can't expect anything else from them yobs! What they need is more discipline. What I say is bring back the birch and national service!' 'They're trouble and always will be, best left alone they are!' 'They are all right really, just normal if you talk to them on their own, it's when they get in gangs that the trouble begins!' And on the basis of this kind of thinking people variously argued about closing the youth centre, excluding the trouble makers, imposing more discipline, introducing epilogues, or using more of 'our own young people' to tame the others.

The other response was made by the staff directly responsible for the work of the centre. I will concentrate on that because it redeemed the situation. We started by making responses of the kind described above and saw they were not getting us anywhere. Then together as 'active participant observers' who saw what happened from different angles we worked out from all our observations that there were three categories of young people in the centre. We called them 'co-operatives' 'hostiles', and 'aggressives'. The co-operatives and the hostiles could live together without violence until the aggressives arrived. Then the hostiles joined the aggressives, became violent, damaged premises and attacked the co-operatives and the staff. The co-operatives disappeared and when they returned for the next club night were aggressive to the staff because they had allowed 'that lot to spoil our club and evening'. Much of this analysis was done through diagrams which showed dramatically just what had been happening, i.e., they became for those involved 'disclosure models' (cf Figure 6). They pictured unmistakably what was happening between the groups.(2)

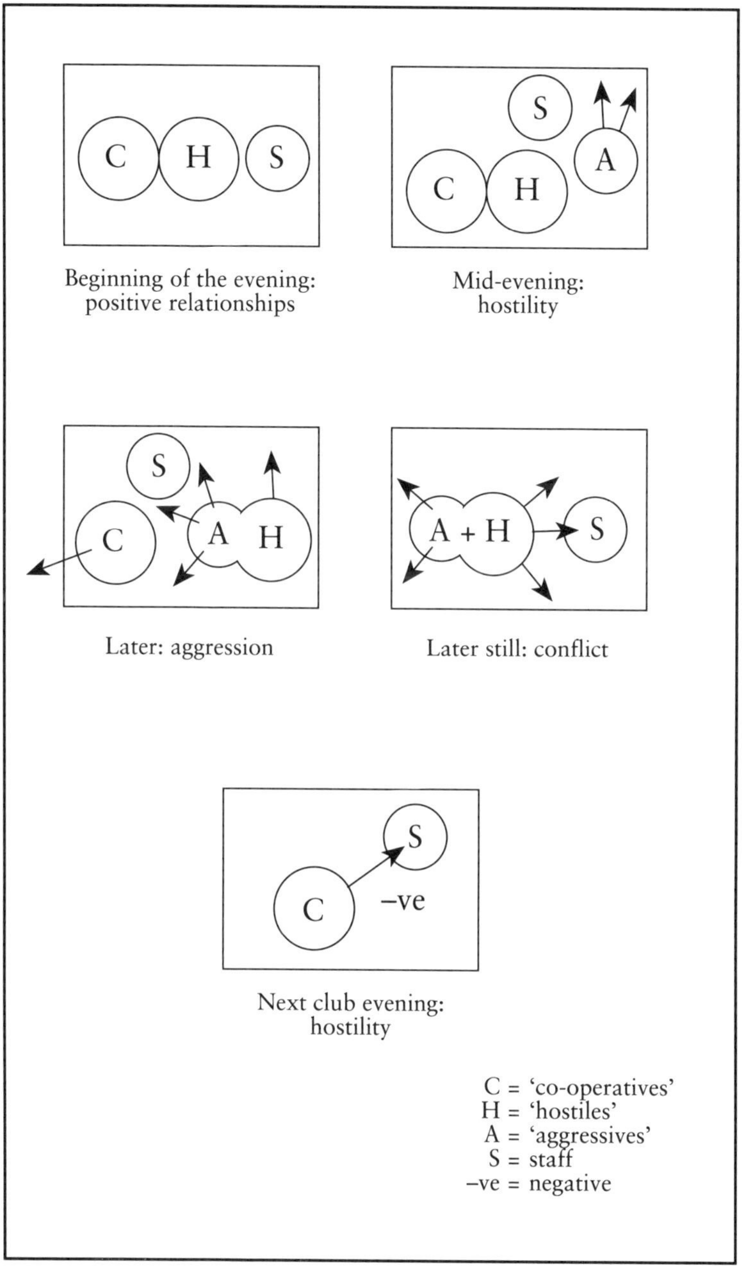


**Figure 6** Inter-group dynamics during a club session

Next we considered the relevance of some research into hostile and aggressive behaviour.[3] We then speculated about the possible causes of aggression:

- It could have resulted from clashes between cultures.
- It could be 'displaced aggression'.
- It could have been aggravated by aggressive and hostile attitudes of the staff.
- It could have been aggravated by permissiveness: some helpers interpreted the non-directive approach as a permissive approach.
- It could have been aggravated by the lack of clearly designated authority to helpers and members.
- It could have been caused by trying to meet too many needs of too many different kinds of people at the same time in the same place.

The implications for the future were then worked out by the staff who arranged that the co-operatives, the hostiles and the aggressives met separately, each subject to clearly defined behaviour boundaries formulated from the analysis and the research findings and imposed unequivocally in a directive and firm manner. The non-directive approach was practised much more effectively within these boundaries. Work started with young people outside the centre in the places where they normally gathered. Success followed some early difficulties, and eventually led to the interchange of members of the groups and to positive interaction between them.

Those responsible for the work of the centre, about twelve in number, had never done this kind of thing before. Only two or three had any relevant professional training and most of them had no academic training at all.

Clubs for the aggressive and hostile (about 250 'skinheads') were based upon the idea that they were most likely to meet the immediate needs of these young people with least danger of outbreaks of aggressive and hostile behaviour if the leader, helpers and members were all members of the 'working class'. A suitable person to act as leader was found, Mr Dan Rodney. We, the youth worker, by now Mr Colin Grant, the Croydon Youth Organizer and I planned the club in close co-operation with him. He recruited members from those who had been displaced from the Centre, found his own helpers, and started a two-night a week club in July 1969. The rules were simple: 'Anyone can come who pays his subs and doesn't do any damage'. The youth worker and I met the leader outside the club for consultations. In the Centre the leader was in control. The youth worker served behind the coffee bar in order to observe what was going on without intruding into the club. (A person behind the bar is not seen as belonging to the club.) This enabled him to help the leader think about the Club. I did not enter the club until the leader invited me. When he introduced me he simply said to the members with a thumbs up sign, 'He's straight, O.K.' I was immediately accepted by those who had previously abused me verbally and physically.

This was a vitally important arrangement. Too often we feel we must work directly with people or leave it to others. We could not work with skinheads. We needed a leader who could. In turn he needed us to help him to think through things, to support him and to help him to relate to the other adults in the Centre and church. The idea worked. The chain link from church to members was creative. There was some aggression and hostility but the leader dealt with it in his own way.

Three cameos illustrate some of the experience of this period. Eventually members of the community club, Axis, and the skinheads met to thrash out some of the problems caused by the damage to property. They were sitting opposite each other. The articulate middle-class members of Axis made carefully argued speeches. The response was in a very different form of communication! Eventually frustrated to breaking point by the mismatch between these ways of talking, one of the skinheads stomped to where the Chairman, the new youth worker, Mr Jim Jones, was sitting, picked him up out of his seat and bawled, 'No one speaks for more than two minutes, that's the rule, right'. Communication started and new relationships were formed.

Eventually the young people who damaged the premises offered to redecorate them. Permission for them to do so was granted by the Trustees, they even gave them the freedom to choose the colours! I raised the question of costs with the young people. 'We'll look after that guv, we know where to get it'. It was clear that they were going to steal it. I remonstrated weakly by saying, 'But it will take a lot of paint'. Their reply was immediate, 'We'll bring it out in bits, leave that to us'. Then plucking up my moral courage I said that we could not be a party to church property being painted with stolen paint. For several nights discussions went on about our respective ethical positions. They saw nothing wrong in taking things from their employers because they said their employers took so much from them. Mutual understanding grew but our respective views on whether it was right to take the paint remained unaltered. Ultimately they broke the deadlock by saying, 'We don't agree, but we'll buy it for your sake'. A high morality, I thought. Grace flowing into the church.

A favourite occupation on Saturday evenings in the autumn of 1968 was to throw billiard balls around. Quite regularly at the end of the evening some members would take balls with them as they left and throw them through the large coloured glass window immediately behind the communion table. As I knelt to start the eight o'clock communion service on a Sunday morning after a particularly harrowing Saturday night, a light flashed from the base of the cross. It was the sun shining on a small jagged piece of glass which had fallen there when the window was broken and had been missed in the clearing up. I still have it. In a moment everything was in place in the context of the ministry and suffering of Christ.

One of the things that these events show is that taking mundane problems seriously can lead to important developments. Therefore, all difficulties, no matter how small warrant thorough consideration. Another thing is the usefulness of questions which enable people to sort out their experience and order their thoughts. In many cases introducing structure into people's thinking is all that is required to enable them to solve their problems. It is particularly important to have facilitating structures such as the problem solving sequence to fall back on when it is difficult to get our minds round things and when feelings are running high.

As the methods proved to be useful I was asked to explain and to demonstrate in small groups how to use them. Gradually these ways of tackling problems became second nature to Parchmore people. They used them to tackle problems when they were active and before they became active. There is a tendency to rely upon solving problems when they are active and to neglect the pre-active and post-active periods when so much can be done to prevent and heal.

I have continued to use the methods, to refine them and to write about them.[4]

# — Chapter Six —
# MONITORING AND EVALUATING

Monitoring and evaluating the work of Parchmore as it evolved was an integral and essential part of the development processes. Adopting an action research[1] approach to my work and the rigours of writing a thesis helped me to evaluate the work more thoroughly than I would otherwise have been able to do. I devised a way of monitoring and evaluating changes for better and worse in relation to purpose. As purpose gives direction to intent and effort I called this form of evaluation 'directional analysis of change'. It is simply not possible to measure the changes in people that I was most concerned to promote: changes for example in their commitment to the well-being of others cannot be quantified. So I had to use changes in behaviour which pointed to the changes I wanted to see. These I called 'behavioural indicators'. Focusing on behaviour was important: it shows what people have/have not translated into action. I defined indicators as follows:

> *An indicator is a symptom of personal or social change which can be observed, classified, assessed and possibly quantified, and which points to changes in people in their attitudes, their ways of thinking, and their relationships which it is necessary to assess but which cannot be measured in exactly the same way because they are not open to direct observation.*[2]

Clusters of indicators were used to assess changes because they were much more reliable than individual indicators.[3] One of the clusters was about 'increased self confidence':

- People increasingly felt able to contribute to the solution of some of Parchmore's problems.
- Increasingly difficult tasks were undertaken.
- People spoke openly of what they really felt and thought.
- People of different cultures and religious convictions came into creative relationships.

This system worked and worked well as did another system which evolved through the Sunbury Conferences. It involved assessing change in relation to purpose through comparing the situation at one period of time with that at another, i.e., through a process of comparison. An example from the 1969 Sunbury Conference will illustrate the method and what at best it produced. The fifty all-age members of the conference spent the Sunday morning considering the changes and developments which had taken place since Sunbury 1968 and the implications for the future. We listed seven aspects of Parchmore on newsprint and the changes that had occurred during the past year. The chart as compiled at the conference is presented in Display 3.

| Different aspects | Changes and Developments since Sunbury '68 |
|---|---|
| The Building | The remodelling of the church and the centre were almost complete and are in use. We now have more extensive premises for activities other than worship. |
| Organization | • More associations of people therefore increased organization necessary.<br>• A Working Party has become necessary to look into our total organization and to facilitate easier working together of the varied groups.<br>• We are more business-like at meetings.<br>• 10.30 Church began in October 1968. |
| Associations of People | • Closing of former 2-night-a-week young people's club.<br>• Centre Club was open 3 nights a week until December. This was a very free and open association for young people. We came face-to-face with hostility and aggression. The Club closed.<br>• January opening of the present Centre Club 2 nights a week. Control, rules, planning very much in the hands of its members through their Committee. There has been development without hostility.<br>• In January, also, the formation of P.Y.E. (Parchmore Younger Element) at its beginning an association of Church-connected young people (but now drawing on a wider circle); meeting regularly on Saturdays, self-programming; members have chosen their own 'Chairman'. (An adult who would normally be called 'Leader') |

**Display 3** Chart used to evaluate changes (continued overleaf)

| Different aspects | Changes and Developments since Sunbury '68 |
|---|---|
| Associations *(cont)* | • Axis has become established and has developed: open to anyone. Membership: 2/3rds older people, 1/3rd younger people. Self-programming.<br>• Retired People's Group.<br>• Thursday mornings.<br>• Play group is developing according to 'Parchmore' methods. Concerned about parents as well as with children.<br>• Coffee after services. |
| Atmosphere | Everything affects atmosphere, sometimes for the good, sometimes not. It has not changed entirely. *How* has it changed? We are more business-like. People feel they can participate in decision-making. More people are putting forward ideas. |
| Church. | • 10.30 Church.<br>• Community Worship once a month. Some people come to this who were not previously Church attendees, therefore the congregation has changed to this degree. |
| People | Our activities, and to a limited extent our Community Services, have brought non-Church people into out Community, not only to use or enjoy our facilities, but also to work in co-operation with Parchmore people; e.g. Centre Club, Axis, Play group. |
| Method | We have tried to make as many groups as possible self-programming and to give everyone concerned in affairs a chance to contribute to decision-making. The senior Department of 10.30 Church has experimented with new educational methods which involve dialogue and immediate communication with the young people. The result: closer contact with them; increasing knowledge about how they think; greater opportunity to show the relevance of Christian faith to their life situations. (This method is known as the Experiential Approach to Christian Education and is the basis of all 10.30 Church educational work.)<br>*(The meeting did not deal with staffing changes).* |

**Display 3** Chart used to evaluate changes (continued from previous page)

When the chart was completed I got the members to reflect on it and study it. One of the members of the conference said, and the others agreed with him, that there were fewer changes to list under 'church' than under any of the other aspects and the changes listed derived from the Christian education programme for children and young people. One member (the Boys' Brigade Captain) said:

> 'New methods have been adopted in the formal education of children and young people which have shown the inadequacy of the Boys' Brigade Bible Class (which was like a service of worship). As a consequence teachers and officers have entered into dialogue with young people, begun to learn how they think and relate the faith to their thinking. In the youth clubs and other activities emphasis is placed upon the value of everyone having the opportunity to take part, to make suggestions and express their ideas.'
>
> 'But in the church people sit in rows and are "talked at". In this situation they do not meet each other nor do they have opportunities to ask questions to clarify meaning or to express their own thoughts.'
>
> 'If new methods of approach are necessary for these other activities why not also for people who attend worship?'

These points were discussed for some time and then I constructed the diagram reproduced in Figure 7 and the members said that it vividly represented how they saw the situation. This diagram played an important part in changes that subsequently occurred and was referred to throughout the remainder of my ministry.

After further discussion it was agreed to put all this and the following suggestions about worship to the special Leaders' Meeting already planned to consider the outcome of the Sunbury Conference.

- Traditional services of worship are of great value but they require supplementing with opportunities to question and discuss.
- Sometimes sermons might be replaced by an open forum or by a dramatic production or by a television programme.

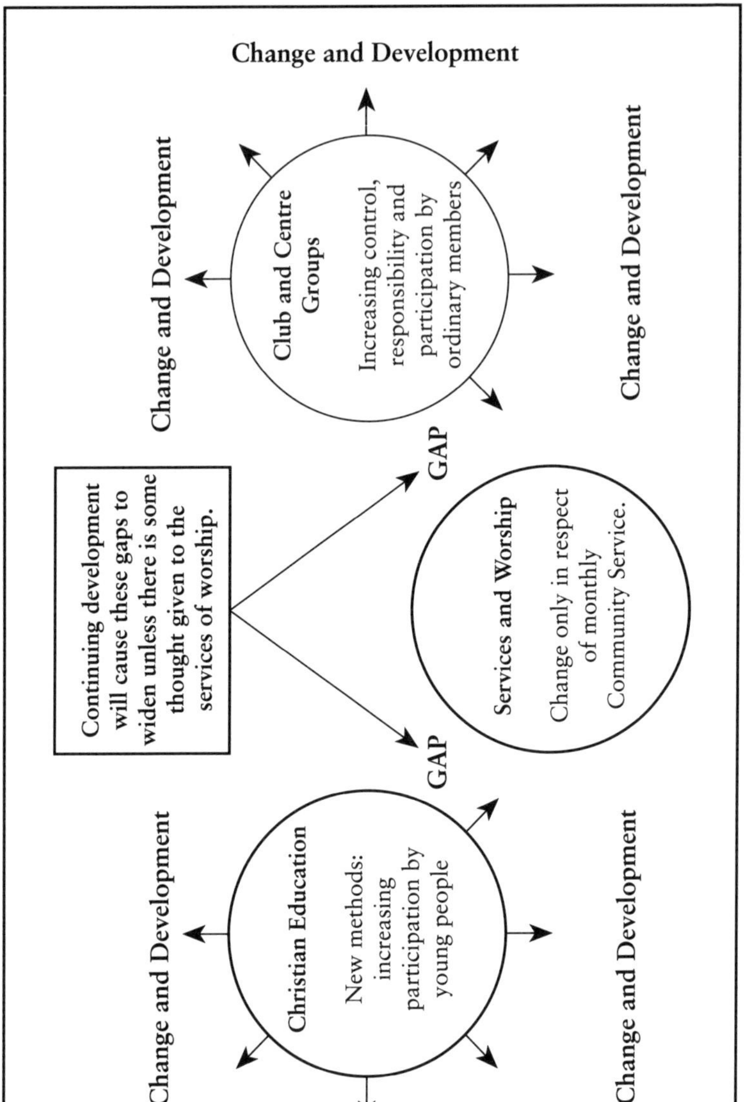


**Figure 7** Widening gaps between church services, christian education and youth and community centre work

- Communion should be more central, i.e., it should be celebrated during the preaching service and not after it.
- Community worship was probably successful because it was based on new educational methods. The members of the Conference said that they needed 'education in the faith' and that opportunities of 'sharing experiences' would help them to relate the teaching of the church to the actual situations in which they find themselves.

Subsequent events proved the enormous value of monitoring developments in this way. Two days later the Leaders got to work on the outcome of the conference. By and large they agreed with the analysis and with the suggestions. But some of them were fearful of changes because the present arrangements suited them and many other people. Their position and feelings were taken very seriously. They were assured that in any new arrangements their needs as well as those of others must be met. Also the Boys' Brigade Officers reassured them by saying that they had feared changes in educational methods but having found the courage to experiment they were now totally convinced of the value of the new approach. Gradually a confidence emerged that the variety of worship needs would be respected and every effort would be made to meet them. All the leaders then gave themselves fully to deciding what action to take. They listed all the needs to be met and appointed a working party representative of the various needs expressed during the meeting to think out ways of implementing changes in worship in order that all these needs be met. The working party of nine people and myself met on three occasions two of which were Saturday mornings. We applied ourselves assiduously to the tasks. We varied in our attitudes to worship and, whilst we were remarkably frank with each other, we were sympathetic towards each others' viewpoint. The meetings were very happy, productive and satisfying occasions. We presented our report to the Leaders' Meeting two months later. It contained fourteen recommendations. The first four recommendations were explicitly on the ways in which the changes should be made:

**Recommendation 1:** That those whose worship and devotional needs are met by the present arrangements should not be unduly deprived through any arrangements made to meet unmet worship needs.

**Recommendation 2:** That the introduction of any new ideas be gradual, i.e., normally not more than two experiments a month. This would leave no less than six services a month unaltered.

**Recommendation 3:** That every effort be made to give people due notice of any different form of services, so that they do not find themselves in a service they would not have attended had they known beforehand what form it was to take. (The thinking behind this was that people should not have new kinds of services 'sprung upon them'. If this occurred they might feel that they had been 'caught' or 'trapped'. Consequently they may react against new services and, because they would not know when another service was planned, they may decide not to attend church at all rather than be 'caught out' again.)

**Recommendation 4:** That as far as possible the people concerned have as much say in the introduction and formulation of new plans as is possible. For example: those who wish to have a devotional Bible study could meet to decide the nature and regularity of the meetings:

- the morning congregation could be invited to complete a simple questionnaire about, say, a 'question and answer' service;
- people should be consulted about any plans the Leaders might have for changes in the pattern of Sunday worship through meetings open to anyone.

The working party advised the Leaders to consult with the people who would be affected by changes rather than legislate for them. These recommendations and ways of implementing them were thoroughly discussed before they were accepted enthusiastically and unanimously. Then, and only then, the Leaders turned to the changes proposed.

Subordinating the 'what of change' to the 'how of change' was right. This had worked in making changes in the Christian education programme and the youth and community work. Whilst these discussions were going on I had a salutary reminder of what could happen if members of the congregation felt threatened by new forms of worship. It occurred during an interview with a life-long member of Parchmore Methodist church with deep family connections with the church. She had visited me to talk about a business matter. The business concluded the conversation somehow fixed on new patterns of worship. The lady, normally extremely polite and retiring, became most irate. She said that she had not come intending to say what was on her mind but as the subject had come up she was going to say it now rather than later. She said that her needs and those of a lot of other people were met by the present services, that she was opposed to these services being changed, that she would boycott any new kinds of services and that if they became a regular part of Parchmore she would leave the church for another. The intense emotional character of this outburst took me by surprise. I felt that I was being blackmailed into resisting change. I thanked the lady for telling me just how she felt and assured her that it was my purpose that Parchmore should meet as many needs for worship and other things as possible. I was not thinking in terms of meeting some needs at the expense of meeting others. This person remained a member of Parchmore and in regular attendance at traditional services. I put it down entirely to the ways in which changes were introduced. She was normally absent from non-traditional services but attended one or two over a period of three years. To my knowledge she did not say anything against new forms of worship and she certainly did not in any way obstruct or oppose their introduction.

The other recommendations were also accepted unanimously. They related to Sunday morning and evening worship, church music, drama in worship and weekday devotional meetings. There is not space here to go into the detail.

All the ideas and recommendations which the leaders meeting approved were put into practice. They were reviewed and evaluated by the leaders and the people at regular intervals and adjustments made as seemed appropriate. The result was that in 1972 there was a varied and balanced programme of worship which met the worship needs expressed by the people. During 1971–72 the establishment of bi-monthly 'Parchmore Family Evenings' was a major breakthrough for Sunday evening worship which was in serious decline. Each service consisted of an informal act of worship for people of any age, followed by a buffet meal and community social activities. These services were extremely popular and attracted large numbers of people, including many teenagers not accustomed to attending worship. Some of them would go out to the toilet (for a smoke) just as they would at the cinema. At first people accustomed to formal worship found this objectionable but after talking it through accepted it. Prayer times were very important and moving. We talked about what we were going to pray about before we prayed. I moved around the 'congregation' discussing prayer items. All kinds of human situations were brought forward for prayer by young and old alike. Discussing them became corporate prayer. After all these years, as I write, I feel again the moving atmosphere generated by these prayer sessions.

Various ad hoc groups of people were involved in planning and organizing other kinds of services. New forms of music were introduced into acts of worship by young people. The adults were as keen on the new songs as the young people and children. A singing group was inaugurated combining choir members and those who had previously sung only in Parchmore concert party productions. Communion services and the other traditional forms of worship took on new meanings. The developments did not cause any faction and only two people regularly absented themselves from non-traditional forms of worship. These people were consistently present at other services and there was no estrangement between them and others on this account. The forms of worship were, in fact, closely related to the natural and different ways in which the people of Parchmore expressed their feelings. The gaps between the three circles first identified at Sunbury were closed. Interestingly the current Parchmore logo, reproduced opposite in Figure 8, has three overlapping circles at the centre of a cross.

**Figure 8** Current Parchmore logo

# — Chapter Seven —
# OVERVIEW AND REFLECTION

## Developments

During the period immediately preceding that described in this part of the book, Parchmore people were experiencing a period of crisis. Many of them foresaw that, unless some radical changes occurred, Parchmore would cease to exist. They themselves could not think of effective ways of dealing with the situation. A scheme to convert their premises into a church, youth and community centre was presented as the solution, the only solution. Although they had no other ideas many Parchmore people had reservations, doubts and suspicions about this proposal which they felt was being imposed upon them. Eventually, however, a majority of Trustees and Leaders agreed to accept the scheme in principle.

Some six years later the attitudes and outlook of the people were very different, as was the working situation. The community centred on Parchmore had found a new lease of life. Together, minister and people had carried out successfully a rebuilding scheme. They had studied and applied non-directive community development approaches to their project and successfully introduced wide-ranging new programmes of church, youth and community work. They had introduced training programmes. They had revised their programmes of Christian education and worship. They had made radical changes in the administrative and organizational procedures to meet the new situation. They felt things were controlled locally by them and those with whom they worked and shared their facilities. They had negotiated the employment of additional staff a full-time youth worker, part-time youth and community workers and a full-time resident caretaker. They had successfully employed two full-time youth workers, Penny Thatcher and Jim Jones but they were unable to replace Jim when he left because of an acute shortage of such people. A man in his mid-twenties, Colin Grant, who had been brought up and trained in youth work in Parchmore, offered to take on the job until he went to college to qualify in youth and community work (he now holds a senior position in this field). Colin had played a leading part in developing the youth and community work, the training programme and in solving the problems of aggressive behaviour in the youth centre (cf. pp53ff). Together, minister and people had also made adequate financial arrangements for the work. They were working with more people from a wider social and religious spectrum than ever before and yet they did not feel they had lost their identity as they had feared they would. They were facing many problems but the despondency had given way to a new confidence. They were able to think, consult and act together (they were more self-determining) and they were able to cope more adequately and creatively with conflict. What had started as a building scheme had become a church and community development project. These changes came about, I believe, directly as a consequence of people working *with* each other rather than *for* each other.

Generally speaking in the 1960s ministers of religion and church leaders worked on the assumption that people needed guidance: for example, they needed to be told what their personal, social and spiritual needs were and how best to meet them; and they needed to be told what they ought to value or what they ought to do for their own good or how they ought to behave. What we did in Parchmore raises serious doubts about the validity of such assumptions. The quite ordinary Parchmore church people did think and act for themselves in complex situations. They did determine and articulate their personal, social and religious needs and find appropriate ways of satisfying them. They did state their aims and select effective methods of achieving them. They did work through plans systematically. They did use their limited membership (around 160 people) and their slender resources to maximum effect. They did organize their affairs in ways appropriate to their situation and their way of life. They did respond positively to change and helped others to do so. They did handle conflict constructively. They did share their facilities and resources with people from other cultural groups. They did help others to feel that Parchmore was 'theirs'. I found I was able to help them to do all these things in a very positive way without telling them what they ought to do or how they ought to do it.

In the process of doing these things individuals and groups in the church and in the neighbourhood of the church increased their competence in working and getting on with other people. They learned more about themselves and others. They learned new ways of tackling old problems. The church people learned more about their faith and they became more conscious of themselves as

Christians and of the needs and feelings of others. They established new relationships with their neighbours. They found new ways of putting some of their beliefs and values into practice. A 'we' feeling emerged in church and neighbourhood groups and between them.

**Working with the parts and the whole**

These developments resulted directly from stimulating and helping people from the church and the community, separately and together, to decide for themselves what their needs were, what they were willing to do to meet them and how best they could organize, plan and act to satisfy them.

This way of working was effective because it was consistently analytical, non-directive and systematic whether we were studying underlying concepts, designing and planning, training, tackling problems or monitoring and evaluating. It was also effective because eventually we used it in relation to every aspect of the work in which we were engaged. The following diagram, Figure 9, helps to bring out the significance of this.

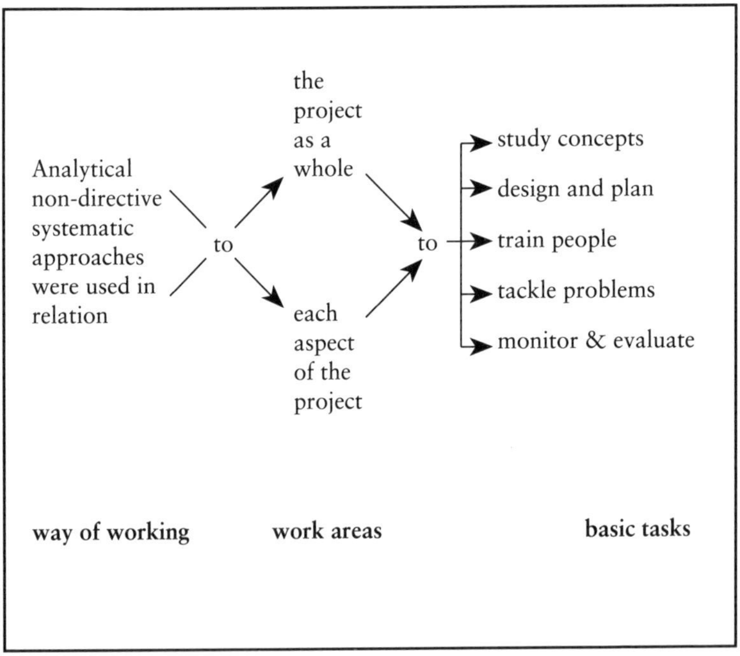


**Figure 9** The way of working used in all work areas to perform basic tasks

This diagram indicates that what we did, in fact, was to work with Parchmore as a system, i.e., a number of parts which form a whole by working together. Some would describe this way of working as systemic and holistic. At the time, however, I did not think of it as such. I only knew that our integrity and that of the work we were doing depended upon us working in the same way with everyone and everything. Therefore the approach we adopted was consistently analytical, non-directive, systematic and systemic.

**Being systematic**

Central to this way of working was the non-directive approach which ensured that the intuitions and feelings as well as the thoughts of all concerned were taken into account. This approach is often associated with a cool, casual and indifferent approach to working with people. There was nothing of this in the way we applied it at Parchmore. Preparation for and follow through of meetings was rigorous. Objectives were defined and the information people needed to participate effectively was carefully and sometimes laboriously gathered and then shared in a manageable way. Much effort went into introducing structure into meetings, series of meetings and projects. This enabled people to think through things together, to work out what they were going to do, to do it and to evaluate it. The structure could be a series of tasks or questions carefully arranged in sequence like those used in problem solving. Good structuring helped people to:

- analyse their problems and accurately identify their needs;
- gather together all relevant information;
- work out alternative courses of action;
- tabulate the advantages and disadvantages of each course of action;
- understand the possibilities inherent in each course of action and the possibilities which they excluded;
- make decisions and act upon them;
- review what they have done and what happened as a consequence;
- make further decisions in the light of their experience and act upon them.

Structures prepared before meetings were offered for use and adopted or adapted; they were not imposed. As people used these to think through things other structures often emerged which led to new patterns of thought. Over-structuring killed the spirit of free thought. Too little structure left thinking woolly and ineffectual. The art was to get the right fit. Records were prepared from full notes taken as meetings proceeded and circulated to all participants as soon after the meeting as possible. Records were not minutes. They were structured accounts of meetings giving an orderly presentation of:

- the overt purposes, objectives, tasks of the meeting;
- any relevant information about the way in which the meeting was conducted;
- any decisions made or conclusions arrived at by the members;
- any of the underlying considerations, arguments, reasons and feelings which led the members to their decisions and conclusions;
- any information about the apparent group processes and the overt interaction of the members necessary for an understandings of whatever happened in the meeting.

These records were greatly valued, they were referred to as 'building blocks'. They enabled one meeting to build on another by obviating the need to go over the same ground and preventing us going round in circles. They put the thinking in order in the context in which it occurred. We devised this form of recording to meet the need for a collective 'memory' of what happened at meetings which could be relied upon. The records helped to keep those unable to attend meetings informed and involved, often another member went through the record with an absent member. Also, they helped us to make the best use of the limited time available for thinking through things together. They set out the thinking of one session so that it could be taken hold of more creatively by all the members of the next one whether they had been at the previous one or not. Two people greatly helped to develop this form of recording and to teach it to others, the late Dorothy Household and Miss Pat Broughton (now Mrs Grant). One of my basic responsibilities, as I noted in the Introduction, was to prime, promote and service this systematic non-directive approach and to make it work. I saw myself as a 'worker' rather than a 'leader'. The overall effect upon most people was very positive. It brought new life. People who had been lukewarm or indifferent to the church became enthusiastically involved. They felt we were getting somewhere. Some, however, found the processes too rigorous and complained about the paper work. Looking back I can see that, like all people learning new ways of doing things, I used the methods in a clumsy manner at times and made mistakes.

Systematic, non-directive action promotes a powerful development process when applied to the stuff of life sensitively and imaginatively as well as analytically. It enables us to work purposefully for things we want and so to effect change within, around and beyond us. It equips us to think creatively, separately and together, for the common good and to make our best contributions to human and spiritual development through religious and secular organizations and their systems. Gradually this approach was written deep into Parchmore people, into the way in which things were done and into the structures of the church and centre. People started to talk with affection and pride about 'the Parchmore way of doing things'. Wherever possible they exported it to other churches and organizations and to such things as school staff meetings.

**Conversions**

Through all this several interrelated conversions were taking place. The buildings were converted. That was reasonably easy to understand although for many of us gutting the beloved church, ripping out the lovely woodwork and removing the beautiful stained glass was heart-breaking, it recalled so many precious memories. We, people and minister, were converted to a new pattern and programme of work far more comprehensive in scope than anything we had done before. This was exciting, frightening and humbling. The increase in the number of organizations was considerable: a five night a week youth centre, a five day a week playgroup, a community club, training groups, a comprehensive Christian educational programme. And the number of people using the church and centre had risen from around 150 a week to one thousand and some of these used it several times a week. Another conversion was that we were working with people from very different cultures and religious backgrounds on equal terms which was exciting but demanding and at times searing. Undoubtedly, however, the most difficult and profound conversion was in the approach to church, youth and community work and in our working relationships. Working *with* rather than *for* people analytically, systematically and systemically, was a big change to make. Doing so with all kinds of people was a great adventure, and at times unnerving. It was harder to grasp than changes to buildings or work programmes. Some of the differences between working *with* and *for* are subtle. And making this change led to changes in our thinking about leadership and theology and in our spirituality. We developed a spirituality appropriate to the way of working and the programme of work. Church people were converted to Church in community and community in Church. People from the community were converted to a new concept of the church and of Christianity in community. I was greatly helped to see these conversions in context by a statement Bishop Stephen Neil made at the World Council of Churches Assembly at Evanston in 1954: 'The true Christian is a man (sic) who has experienced three conversions to Christ, to the Church and to the World'.(1)

We were all at different stages of conversion in understanding and growth. The coherence of approach and method that had held Parchmore together for several decades had gone. A new approach and a new theology were emerging but had not yet matured. None of us were fully converted, some were not converted at all. But we, converted, part converted and unconverted, were on the way together. We were living in an expanding secular and religious world of thought and action aimed at human and spiritual well-being of the people of Parchmore and Thornton Heath.

**Thoughtful action**

As I come to the end of this account one of the things that most impresses me is the point I made in the Introduction, the thinking we did together. I am amazed at the breadth, depth and intensity of it and the way in which it was sustained over such a long period of time. People of all ages, Christians and non-Christians, engaged in it separately and together on a wide range of subjects to do with human and spiritual well-being and development. We thought, worked things out, put them into practice and then thought and thought again. We had an enormous appetite for rigorous thinking that issued in action. I realized just how important it was that it issued in action when I was working on the records of the 1967 Teach-In and the Workshop. Some people had said that they badly needed to see Christians effectively at work in their community. For years they had heard from the pulpit what Christianity could do for society, and what it was doing here and there, now they wanted to see it for themselves and to be involved in what happened. Without it their connection with the Church would have become gradually more tenuous.

A lot of excitement and satisfaction resulted from the enormous amount of work involved in working in this way. It has to be done in development work: it is not an optional extra for work addicts. Churches and other development agencies simply must budget for it instead of leaving it as a hidden cost to be paid privately by dedicated workers and their families. Without it secure foundations for the new Parchmore would never have been laid. As there is only so much thinking time available it is important to use it on the essentials. Thinking things through together made the project what it became. All the significant developments derived from the thinking processes set in a context of prayer.

**My Withdrawal**

My appointment as the minister at Parchmore concluded on the 31st August 1972. I felt that a phase of my ministry had been completed and that this was the time to hand over to someone else.

I had carried out a thorough evaluation of the work for my doctoral thesis. This showed that the non-directive approach works and that it had widespread implications for the work of people in the church – lay, religious and ordained – who wish to promote betterment in church and community. Having done this I saw the need to test it out in churches of other denominations. And that is what I did.

I am still drawing upon what I learnt through Parchmore. To Parchmore I owe a great debt. Being its minister dramatically changed the shape of my life and ministry and set me on a road upon which I am still travelling. A deep sense of gratitude wells up. But thankfully it was not the end of my ministry to and through Parchmore. So far all of my successors and the Parchmore people have graciously allowed me the privilege of making contributions to the on-going work. Contributing to this book is one of them. Thank you very much Parchmore past, present and future for all you have contributed and continue to contribute to me and my ministry.

## — Postscript —
# PARCHMORE IN CONTEXT

**A local project and a national movement**

As you read what I have written you might well come to the conclusion that the developments at Parchmore were entirely due to local initiative and effort. That is not so. Parchmore is an outstanding example of what can be achieved locally through connexional collaboration. It models the action from above which promotes development from below. To set Parchmore in context things need to be said about other contributions to its development even though the whole story is beyond the scope of this book.

**Circuit support**

From the outset Parchmore had the good fortune to have the unwavering support of the Croydon circuit of which it was a member. Superintendents, staff and circuit officers ensured that the minister of Parchmore did not have pastoral responsibilities for other churches, of which there were five. They took a keen interest in the developments and monitored the project. They supported ministers through many tough periods. They affirmed the work and rejoiced in the progress. It was humbling to receive such support. I think particularly of my superintendents, the late John Gibbs and Brynmor Salmon. The circuit and some of the churches found money towards the project. Some people from the circuit attended workshops during my ministry and Shirley, the largest of the churches, asked me to run a training course in church and community development for their minister and leaders. Shirley also seconded Miss Frances Truscott and Mr Leslie Campion to help to establish the new comprehensive educational programme in the sixties. Terry Young, a member of the Shirley church who was training at Handsworth Theological College spent most of his vacations and his placements at Parchmore for a period of two years. All this genuine interest, assistance and involvement was enormously encouraging and helpful. It meant the circuit worked with Parchmore realistically. Another thing which the circuit did at the outset was to undertake to appoint ministers and other staff to Parchmore who were committed to the non-directive approach and had the ability to promote it. Parchmore has done the same in appointing youth and community workers.

For over twenty years all those appointed to be full-time workers at Parchmore have attended Avec* courses. Holding to this policy over a period of twenty-seven years has facilitated growth through continuity: ministers and workers have built on the work of their predecessors. Consequently, developmental processes are now deeply embedded in the church and the community. This simply could not have been achieved had each new appointment introduced fundamental changes of direction.

**The Greater London Youth and Community Service**

Regional and national support from the Methodist Church reinforced that of the circuit. The Joseph Rank Benevolent Trust and the London Mission Committee helped to finance the building. The London Mission, with the backing of the 1964 Methodist Conference, set up an organization to service and support the work of the Ten Centre Scheme and to offer in service training to lay and ordained people, engaged in youth and community work in Methodist churches. It was known as The Greater London Youth and Community Service of the Methodist Church. Full time staff were appointed Terry Walton, and then at various times, Eric Murray, Anthony White and Malcolm Dick. An organizational base and training centre with residential accommodation was established in King's Cross Methodist Church.

From about 1967 onwards and, I think into the 'eighties, under the aegis of King's Cross, the youth workers, community workers and ministers of the centres met regularly for half day sessions, residential conferences, and self-training sessions. Ministers and workers shared experiences, acted as work consultants to each other, tackled common problems, studied the practice, theory and theology of community development work. I still have the report of a conference of ministers of the Ten Centres and the King's Cross staff held at The Friars, Aylesford in 1972 which I led. We teased out the nature of community development; we explored the relationship between the centres, the community and the Methodist Church; we examined the roles of ministers and workers; we studied the organizational implications of community development; and we got very excited as we discussed the distinctive theology of

---

* *Avec, an ecumenical service agency for church and community development was inaugurated in 1976, by Dr George Lovell and Miss Catherine Widdicombe.*

this kind of work. We became a community of reflective practitioners. One of the great advantages of this community was that we could explore any and all subjects and our hopes and fears honestly and openly with impunity. It was a source of moral, technical and spiritual support as we pioneered church and community development work. Sadly King's Cross is now long closed but it made many impressive contributions to Parchmore.

**The Board for Lay Training**

Alongside all this a national movement in the Methodist Church had a great influence upon me, Parchmore and the promotion of church and community development. It was the formation in the early 'sixties of the Board for Lay Training of the Methodist Church and the appointment of Dr Pauline Webb as its Director. Divergent views about the nature and content of lay training and its relationship to ministerial training created an impasse in the work of this Board. Eventually, in 1970, it was decided to set up task groups to concentrate on disciplines which had contributions to make to the training of lay workers and ministers. By then the Board was committed to the interrelated training of ministers and lay workers. Strongly influenced by the 1968 Gulbenkian Report, *Community Work and Social Change: The Report of a Study Group on Training*, the Board set up a Community Development Group. Other groups focused on adult Christian education, vocational training, leadership training institutes or sensitivity training, sociology. The community development group published some important papers and made profound contributions to Parchmore, to action research into church and community development and to the inauguration of Avec.

**The Methodist Church and community development**

Another national movement profoundly influenced the development of church and community development in the Methodist Church. It grew out of the emphases in the 1960s on youth and community work, open youth work in church centres and detached work in the community. Around 1970 the late Douglas Hubery, whilst he was the General Secretary of the Methodist Youth Department, set up an inter-departmental youth committee working party on the church and community development. After a lot of research and wide-ranging discussion a report was presented to the 1973 Methodist Conference stating the importance of the theory and practice of community development to church work and advocating the setting up of ecumenical in-service training programmes. Conference accepted the report and gave directions for its implementation and for the further study of the theology of community development. The work done by this committee and the official recognition it gained gave enormous impetus to church and community development.

Without these regional and national developments it is doubtful whether Parchmore and other centres would have been possible. They affirmed, validated and authorized church and community development work and they provided moral support, technical back up, consultancy help and in-service training for workers. Equally, without the work done in centres such as Parchmore these support and service arrangements would not have had the same significance. In fact local workers made significant contributions to the regional and national movements. There was little patronage in these movements because they had evolved not only from considering the approaches of community development but from using them. They were products of the process which they modelled. By nature and structure, therefore, they were collaborative engendering dialogue between people engaged at all levels. Like all such arrangements they broke down from time to time but by and large they created a context which enabled local workers to give of their best locally, regionally and nationally and for regional and national workers to make their best contributions to local action.

**The non-directive approach**

The Battens contrasted the non-directive approach with the directive approach towards people. They described the directive approach in this way: 'It is the essence of this approach that the agency and its worker think, decide, plan, organize, administer and provide for people'.[1] Agencies and workers using a directive approach provide for what they think the people need. They also decide what they think people ought to value, believe, do for their own good and the patterns of behaviour they think they should adopt. They then seek in various ways to get people to adopt these values, practices, beliefs and patterns of behaviour. Some do it by selling, guiding, and persuading; others convince or convert people by maximising the advantages and minimizing the disadvantages or by offering inducements. It can be done by bargaining with people from unassailable positions of advantage or by indoctrinating them.

From the beginning I was, however, quite clear that there are times when it is necessary and appropriate to provide for people by directive action. There are occasions, such as emergencies, when it is not possible for the people to think and act constructively and realistically for themselves.(2) In such circumstances directive action is essential but this must not be confused with manipulation and indoctrination. These methods are quite different, they deceive and distort. They may well be effective ways of getting people to do what the church or worker wants them to do, but it is difficult for me to imagine situations or circumstances in which they would be legitimate ways of dealing with people.

Some people thought that the non-directive approach was akin to the permissive approach. In this approach the agency or worker does not place any constraint upon people. All beliefs and values are acceptable and may be expressed in any way whatsoever. So, for me, the permissive approach was the antithesis of the directive approach. Others saw the non-directive approach as a mid-way point on a directive permissive scale or continuum. Yet others saw it as a synthesis of the directive and permissive approaches. For me it was neither. Nor was it to be confused, as it often was, with non-direction or non-directional.(3) Those who use the non-directive approach facilitate and encourage people to determine the direction in which they wish to go and the purposes they wish to achieve in such a way that the people have opportunities to develop themselves. Also, non-directive workers have their own purposes; they are not directionless workers. In fact it is a positive and dynamic activity promoted by non-directive workers who:

- try to strengthen incentives for people to act when these are weak by stimulating them to discuss their needs in the hope that they will come to see them more specifically as wants;
- help by providing information, if people need it, about how similar groups have organized for action;
- help people systematically to think through and analyse the nature and causes of any problem they may encounter in the

course of their project, and to explore the pros and cons of each and every suggestion for solving it;

- help by suggesting sources from which the group may be able to obtain any material help or technical advice in addition to what they can provide for themselves.[4]

Helping people in these ways introduces structure into the processes of discussion and decision-making. This structure helps people to think more systematically in the light of all the available information. Helping people to structure their thinking and to learn to think more systematically I saw to be one of my primary responsibilities.

For me the non-directive approach is the principal tool of community development which is variously described as a programme, a method, a philosophy and a process. Community development was to me an educational process by which people change themselves and their behaviour and acquire new skill and confidence through working collaboratively. I was deeply committed to promoting this process through getting people from the local church and its neighbourhood working together for the inter-related development of the secular and religious communities to which they belonged. I felt that I could commit myself as a Christian minister to these approaches and processes because they:

- help people to develop or mature and provide opportunities for educating and influencing people without directing them;
- help the emergence of we feelings;
- enable people to make that contribution to their own growth and development which cannot be made by anyone else;
- promote self-induced change which, in general, is superior to imposed change;
- stimulate people to take into account as many factors as possible which relate to their welfare and development and that of others;
- acknowledge that in working with people to achieve material or human change, processes, methods and attitudes are as important as aims and ends;
- enable all available expertise to be used and people to accomplish more with their limited resources;

- assume that people are more likely to take responsibility for the consequences of their own decisions and for the development of those things which they have planned or organized for themselves than for those things which have been decided, planned or organized for them;
- provide Christians with opportunities to grow and mature;
- value individuals as Jesus did;
- work and communicate with different kinds of people as Jesus did;
- assist people to improve their social, spiritual and physical environments which, according to the Bible, are God ordained tasks;
- emulate Christ's servant ministry;
- continue the biblical search for ideal community.

**Continuing work**(5)

During my ministry at Parchmore I had carried out a thorough evaluation of the work we had done and wrote it up as a doctoral thesis. This showed that the non-directive approach works and that it had widespread implications for people in the church lay, religious and ordained who wish to promote betterment in church and community. Having done this I saw the need to test out this approach in churches of other denominations. I had become involved in an action research project designed to do this by Miss Catherine Widdicombe whilst she was on the Battens' course in 1970. It was known as Project 70–75(6) and it involved working with an ecumenical team to test out the approach with the clergy and laity of sixteen churches and seven denominations. In September 1972 I became a full-time member of that team. Project 70–75 led to the establishment of Avec, an ecumenical service agency for church and community development work in 1976. I was the director of this agency until 1991 and then I was the research worker until 1993. During this period seven and a half thousand presbyteral and diaconal ministers, religious and lay people used Avec services in one way or another. They represented seven denominations. Most of them came equally from the Anglican, Methodist and Roman Catholic churches. The staff did in-depth work studies with 3,500 of these people who were involved in courses, projects and consultations and imbibed the non-directive approach to church and community development which we were promoting. Many of these people are now in positions of authority within education, the Church and community work and are exerting considerable influence on policy, training and development. One series of courses was for people working at regional and national level, i.e., bishops, abbots, chairmen of districts, religious superiors and generals, etc. In addition I have worked in Ireland and with the Church overseas for example in West Africa and Zimbabwe. There is clear evidence that this work has had considerable influence on the thinking, practice and policy of the Church in the United Kingdom, especially the Church of England, and the Methodist and Roman Catholic Churches. It all grew out of Parchmore and I still draw upon what we did together.

My work in this field continues. A Leverhulme Emeritus Fellowship will enable me in the first year or so of my becoming an active supernumerary minister to reflect on and analyse the impact of all this work, to tease out some of its implications and to discuss them with people active in church and community work.

Who could have imagined what was to flow from Parchmore? I could not. I continually thank God for it.

# NOTES AND REFERENCES

## Chapter One: Becoming one of the Ten Centres

1. I have described these problems briefly in my book, *Human and Religious Factors in Church and Community Work* (1982) (Grail Publication) pp14ff.

2. ibid p15.

3. *An Action Research Project to Test the Applicability of the Non-Directive Concept in a Church, Youth and Community Centre Setting.* (Institute of Education, University of London, 1973)

4. There is a note of the development of my subsequent understanding of the non-directive approach in *Diagrammatic Modelling: An Aid to Theological Reflection in Church and Community Development Work* (An Avec Publication) which I wrote in 1980.

5. Oxford University Press, 1967. Now out of print but the first six chapters have been re-printed in *The Non-Directive Approach* by T R and M Batten (An Avec Publication, 1988).

6. op.cit.p11.

7. Throughout the time that I was at Parchmore I worked at the practice theory and the theology and just before I left in 1972 I published a book about both aspects. *The Church and Community Development: An Introduction* (Grail Publications and Chester House Publications, 1972) sets out the ideas and beliefs underlying my work at Parchmore during 1966-72. Also I described my position in an article contributed to the *Expository Times* (LXXXIII No. 2, November 1971) entitled 'The Church and Community Development'. It was later published in a collection of articles in *The Social Sciences and the Churches* edited by C.L. Mitton (T & T Clark, 1972).

8. I have discussed the importance of differentiating between purposes and objectives and a way of doing so in *Human and Religious Factors* pp46ff.

9. cf Lovell, George (1972 revised 1980) *The Church and Community Development: An Introduction* (Grail Publications and Chester House Publications) pp 33ff and Lovell, George

(1982) *Human and Religious Factors in Church and Community Work* (Grail Publications) pp 12ff.

### Chapter Two: Thinking out basic underlying concepts

1. *Voluntary Social Services Handbook and Directory* (The National Council of Social Services, First Printed 1928, Revised Edition: November 1964; Reprinted 1965).
2. An Occasional Paper was published describing the conference in detail: *In Community: A Report of the Parchmore Road Methodist Church, Youth and Community Centre Residential Conference at Sunbury, March 22–24th 1968.*
3. This was taken from a very helpful publication: *Salty Christians: A Handbook for Lay Training Courses*, Hans Ruedi Weber (Published by the Department on the Laity, World Council of Churches, November 1962).
4. Garfinkel, Harold (1959) 'Aspects of the Problem of Common Sense Knowledge of Social Structures' in *Transactions of the Fourth Congress of Sociology* (1959) pp5 1 65.

### Chapter Three: Orientation and Training

1. I described the receiving and giving of consultancy help in an article in *Crucible* October/December 1978: 'Experiences of Working With Other People on Their Work'.
2. Lovell, George (1972 Revised 1980) *The Church and Community Development: An Introduction.* (Grail Publications and Chester House Publications)
3. *Working With People* (A Parchmore Paper, 1971).

### Chapter Four: Designing and Planning

1. cf *Report of the Special Committee on Church Relationships* published by the Boys' Brigade, Brigade House, Parsons Green, London SW6, 1967.

### Chapter Five: Problem solving

1. See Lovell, George and Widdicombe, Catherine (1978 reprinted 1986) *Churches and Communities: An approach to development*

*in the local church* (Search Press) pp145 and 135ff for other examples of the use of this problem solving method which we owe to T R Batten.

2. I have discussed this in *Human and Religious Factors* pp29ff.

3. We found, for example, that some research had demonstrated that some young people are least aggressive when they are not permitted to do certain things but not punished when they do. And that it is greatest when permitted and punished. We had been not permitting and punishing. cf Argyle. *Psychology and Social Problems* (Science Paperbacks, 1964, Ch. 4).

4. I illustrate and discuss problem solving in *Analysis and Design: A Handbook for Practitioners and Consultants in Church and Community Work* (Burns and Oates, 1995).

**Chapter Six: Monitoring and evaluating**

1. Action research involves continuously assessing work done for what can be learnt from it and using whatever is learnt from doing so to inform future decisions and action. For a fuller description see my booklet *Human and Religious Factors in Church and Community Work* pp52ff.

2. My doctoral thesis, p93.

3. op cit p374ff.

**Chapter Seven: Overview and reflection**

1. cf Expository Times Vol 72 p121.

**Postscript: Parchmore in context**

1. Batten T R and M (1988) *The Non-Directive Approach* (see reference 5, Chapter 1) p89.

2. cf op cit., Chapter 3 'Factors Affecting Choice'.

3. op cit., p11.

4. op cit., p13f

5. Aspects of some of the subsequent developments are described briefly in Lovell, George (1982) *Human and Religious Factors in Church and Community Work* (Grail Publication) pp 17ff

and Lovell, George and Widdicombe, Catherine (May 1987) *Our Church and Community Development Stories* (Avec) and Lovell, George *Analysis and Design: Ways of Realising the Learning Potential in Church and Community Work* (Avec 1992 Annual General Meeting).

6. A book was published about this project, Lovell, George and Widdicombe, Catherine (1978 reprinted 1986) *Churches and Communities: An approach to development in the local church* (Search Press)

# Part Two

## It All Began to Happen

*– The Ministry of the Revd Garth Rogers 1972–77*

# IT ALL BEGAN TO HAPPEN

*Garth Rogers 1972–77*

The 'Ten Centre' Programme of the Greater London Youth and Community Service of the Methodist Church was a grand scheme to provide premises and workers for youth work in strategic areas of London. In 1964 I had been invited to the South London Mission to work at the Manor Methodist church in South Bermondsey. They had become involved in the development of youth work in old premises and the beginnings of realization that work in the community was no longer just an option but an absolute necessity. During that time I began to explore, with others, different methods of working and when in 1970 I was invited to St Peter's, Gillingham in the Medway Towns, which had been designated as one of the ten Youth and Community Centres, I saw the opportunity to develop that thinking at work.

I now found myself involved with other ministers and youth workers in training and consultative sessions, and here I was introduced to the work of T R Batten on community development. It seemed just the process I was looking for in relation to Youth Centre and Church work. In common with many ministers and church workers in the 1960s I had suffered an increasing confusion over the role of the ministers and the function of the Church. It seemed increasingly that the clergy were being marginalized or having to find new roles which were of some use in the community. I had struggled with this in Bermondsey without being aware of the movements that were taking place in church community work and of other increasing demands on church premises by communities looking for premises in order to establish community activities. The introduction to the work of Batten and others gave me insight into a method that made sense of the struggles to be with the community and Tenants Associations in Bermondsey and, perhaps, more significantly for me, a real role and function for the minister. The autocratic, authoritarian leadership of past days was not for me but I had received no training or insight into any other way of being a minister or a leader. No wonder that perhaps I went over the top and began to believe that the method was also the message. My years at Parchmore gave a clearer perspective and a firmer intent. My time at Gillingham was to be a short one, for one Tuesday morning I received a telephone call from the Chairman of the Methodist District in South-East London. "Would you like to go back to London?" he asked. George Lovell at Parchmore was leaving to work in a Church and Community Development Research project and a successor was being sought. Of course I had come to know George and his work at Parchmore with the team of ministers and youth workers and my immediate response was "yes please". Parchmore was, in my estimation, the Flag Ship of the Ten Centre Programme and George Lovell the acknowledged leader in the community development processes now being explored within the Methodist Church. Events followed swiftly and I was invited to Parchmore to meet local people and church people and the rest of the ministerial staff.

**Falling into place**

Much of the work at Parchmore has been recorded by George Lovell and others and his memories are based upon those records. My memories are based not upon written records but upon lasting impressions and therefore may differ in style and sometimes in perspective.

My first visit to Parchmore was both fascinating and depressing. The church in 1972 bore all the signs of people who had lived and worshipped and worked together and found in their relationships a hope not only for survival but for growth. Little reference was made to any possibility of decline or closure yet there were feelings of tiredness and apparently of inadequacy. A great deal had been achieved and the effort had been considerable. They were now beginning to feel tired and perhaps some of the earlier plans had not yet come to realization. Before looking at these feelings and what people did with them it is important to note that what would be seen as problems in most church communities were seen by many of the people at Parchmore as opportunities to be explored. The frustrations experienced were those of a growing, living organism. Clearly as the work had developed the church community had been much concerned in developing work with young people and with those who lived around the church who could be termed the community. The aims of the project had been clearly worked out but the realization of those aims was hindered by lack of co-operation with Education Authorities and Social Service Committees. The church in its youth and community work was not in equilibrium. The friction still existed between those who used Parchmore for their religious needs and those who saw it as a Youth and Community Centre. The Church congregation was growing in strength but the youth work was at a low ebb.

On that first visit to Parchmore the story began to unfold. The Youth Centre built in the lower area of the church was showing signs of use but also of considerable abuse. I was told horror stories by youth workers of lights going out in the Centre and snooker balls being used as invisible, but deadly, missiles. There was no full-time youth worker and considerable gloom about the possibility of attracting anyone to work in the Centre. The Club at that time was being run by part-time workers. They were all committed and were maintaining the Youth Centre against considerable odds.

Community work consisted of a playgroup that ran itself and an attempt at a luncheon club was struggling to be born. The church people believed firmly that the future of the church lay in the development of the whole project and there was no attempt whatsoever to withdraw and to attempt to re-establish the old patterns of church life. The groundwork of church Weekends and many working groups had laid a solid foundation and the project was owned and valued by the church people. I was left in little doubt of the kind of minister that people wanted and one incident made this absolutely clear on that first visit. I was climbing the stairs accompanied by the Boys' Brigade Captain. The history of the Boys' Brigade at Parchmore was a long and successful one and it could be said that they were the mainspring of the church's youth work for many generations. The captain was proudly informing me of this past and showing me the hall upstairs used by the Brigade and other organizations. During the tour he broached the subject of leadership. There was a statement of intent, 'We don't want a minister here who tells us what to do' he said 'We have got used to deciding things together!' Evidently I must have responded in the way which made sense to him and to others for I heard soon after the visit that I would be going to Parchmore Road in the Croydon Methodist circuit in September 1972.

My excitement about the appointment was in some way muted by the knowledge that after the first six years, and various attempts to provide youth leadership, the project was without a youth worker and was at a dangerous and difficult stage. There had been various youth workers full-time, but for one reason or another none of them had stayed the course. It was part of the original plan that the Youth Centre should be staffed by a full-time youth worker and various part-timers. Relationships with the Borough Youth Officers had not produced another full-time appointment and the Centre was under-used. I had been told of the problems as the users of the Centre changed from a white club to an increasing black majority and the Management Committee, which was hopefully representative of the other Church denominations in Thornton Heath. I was also aware that already other designated churches in the 'Ten Centre' programme had started the process of disengagement. Many had not come to terms with the cost of open youth work and premises which had been opened with great hope had now suffered during the process of establishing clubs and other centres. Methodists were increasingly unwilling to see these grand new buildings used in such a way. There was also the difficulty of attracting professional youth workers as the question of open or closed youth work was explored. There were many who believed that we should care for our own young people and through that care establish the future membership of the Church. Open youth work was risky and dangerous both in terms of property and people and yet there was the belief that the mission of the Church demanded an open-door policy. There had been various attempts at establishing community groups within the Centre. Some of these had been successful, in fact the Axis Club for people in the church and their friends from the community, was a considerable step forward in community use of the premises. The Coffee Club had been established and the plans had been made for a Lunch Club, but as yet the church had still to discover a new pattern of life and caring in the local community and to establish work outside the Parchmore Centre. The resolve at Parchmore remained firm and a programme of work to achieve strategic goals was embarked upon.

Things slowly began to fall into place and an amazing snowballing of events and opportunities began which resulted in a major increase in staff and activity within the Centre. These stories are told later but the first problem to be tackled was the appointment of a full-time youth worker. A group was set up to explore the role of the minister in relation to a youth worker and to take appropriate action to ensure adequate staffing at the Centre. A plan of action was worked out to attempt to establish relationships and to point out the importance of a full-time youth worker appointment in the Parchmore Centre. A visit was due at Parchmore from the President of the Methodist Conference. His visit was taken as an opportunity to bring together the various Local Councillors, the Borough Youth Officers and Methodist representatives. The meeting with the President was a productive one and the work at Parchmore was affirmed with the result that the Borough, both in its officers and in its councillors, put a great deal of effort into achieving the appointment of a full-time worker. Eventually this resulted in the appointment of Sylvan Eastmond a black youth worker trained by the YMCA.

The need for a community worker had been appreciated and the appointment of a part-time worker, Rebecca Brown, had resulted. The continued development with Rebecca's leaving the project resulted in the appointment of Christine Morrison who had grown up at Parchmore and who had gone away to train as a teacher. On return she decided not to teach but to look for opportunities in community work. Parchmore was also at that point looking for such an appointment and the two coincided with Christine being made Parchmore's first full-time community worker. Work and programmes began to multiply. Involvement with unemployed young adults began through a young man who had grown up at Parchmore, Nigel Spalding. He became the leader of a work programme which at one time employed twenty-seven young people. The job creation scheme at Parchmore developed not only into a work programme which cared for our people in their homes, a building project which could undertake small building programmes and gardening teams but also into an educational scheme where young people were helped with social skills and in making out job applications. Many of the young people who came to us on the first scheme eventually found their way into full-time work and in fact the criteria and success of the scheme was not that we kept people in the work teams but that they left us and found full-time occupations.

As the minister, I found myself swept along with an increasing speed in the multiplication of groups and activities. Life was a feverish round of activity with little time for reflection as something new seemed to happen every week. The lunch club for the elderly at last became a reality staffed by members of the church. Summer play schemes began and many other groups developed through the work of Christine. To hold all these mushrooming projects together the Community Council, which had been created in the early years of Parchmore's development, began to discover a new role for itself and a new importance for its existence. At this Council representatives from the Church and all other groups within the Community Centre met to consult and to make decisions which affected the common life. The process of communication between groups was proving difficult and many attempts were made to find effective means of communication. A great deal of pastoral work was undertaken by the minister and community worker in an attempt to maintain communications with all groups. The networking process of communication was established as being perhaps the only viable means of keeping everyone involved. In this the minister, the community worker, and the youth workers all played their part, informal conversations and pastoral care were seen as the way of informing and keeping people in touch with each other. This expanded into the community where Street Wardens were appointed and they became carriers of information. Newsletters were published, handbills put out and reports for committees made available, but there were still people who either did not know or had not read, or had forgotten what was happening in the whole of the Centre.

It is important to note that as the new work developed the older organizations continued. The Boys' Brigade and Girl Guides and a Saturday Youth Club for members of these organizations existed alongside the open youth work. The Playgroup continued to flourish and gradually began to see itself as part of the community work. Church Fellowship Groups and Working Groups maintained the life of the Christian community. Although already heavily outnumbered by users of the Centre they took pleasure from the increasing activity.

The time came for Christine Morrison to move on and she was replaced by her mother, Diane Morrison, the post now being funded, but as yet inadequately, by the Social Services Department of the Borough. So partnership both in youth work and social caring had developed and was firmly established. The pieces had fallen into place but it is perhaps worth stopping for a moment to reflect with the benefit of hindsight. A nagging question kept recurring to me about the use of my time as a minister and the aim of the whole project. I did not at that time see community development or open youth work as a method or means for mission to give people the good news of Jesus Christ. I had accepted the 'sixties version of mission that to do the work with no strings or conditions attached was to offer the cup of water and that in itself was enough. New people did join the church attracted by the vibrant life of Parchmore but that was not the aim of the project. There was, on reflection, a real danger of becoming a very good Community Centre which had very little to do with the development of the Christian community and the mission of the Kingdom of God.

What I realize now was happening was the beginning in me of a new concept of God's Kingdom. I had been very much a church-based minister making ventures into the community and finding ways for the community to use the premises and the church. Now I began to see that God was working in the lives of people in the community in their relationships, in their social programmes, and in their work. The church was part of this whole arena of God's activity. He had created the whole world and not just the church. Activities which took place in the community could demonstrate His presence and part of our role was to interpret that presence and point to it to see signs of God's Kingdom in the lives of people. Another example was the language used in worship in the sanctuary upstairs at Parchmore. This to a large extent was unintelligible to the majority of users of the Centre but Parchmore had become a real meeting place between the community and its needs and concerns and the church with its offer of life in Christ. The language did begin to change in worship and a new openness in terms of community worship, which had begun many years before, began to show its effect.

It is time now to look at the stories of development in a little more detail.

### The Youth Centre

Progress at the Youth Centre had been slowed down by the lack of a full-time worker and had been maintained by a small group of dedicated part-time workers. One of these, Dan Rodney, had been totally committed to the project and had established relationships with young people which very few others had begun to imitate. Dan had been there for many years and had grasped many opportunities but now as new staff were appointed, and particularly with the appointment of a full-time youth worker, difficulties and problems arose between the old staff and their views and those of the new. This spilled over into tension and a situation in which all the white members of the Centre felt threatened by newcomers who mainly were members of the black community which was an increasing percentage of the population of Thornton Heath.

When Sylvan Eastmond became the first full-time youth worker in my time at Parchmore these problems were perhaps identified and explored for the first time. As Christians we were concerned to attempt all ways of integrating the two groups but our ideal was sorely tried and eventually a different strategy had to be employed.

In 1974 there were many points of difference which seemed to be irreconcilable. Music was a major source of discontent with many liking the heavy beat music and the emergence of a new West Indian culture in music. Disco nights were fraught, with trouble only a minute away. It became quite customary on Friday evenings for the Centre to be surrounded by police cars and the young people searched as they left the Centre. This was not an idle attempt by the police for in our own searches at night many weapons were discovered on people carrying them into the Centre. In retrospect we were extremely fortunate that violence never broke out within Parchmore but increasingly neighbours were concerned and the police involved in disturbances after the Youth Centre closed.

As a result of our attempt to provide a meeting place for young people, and with the best intentions, we were now in the midst of having to come to terms with cultural differences as well as outright acknowledged racial prejudice. How to deal with this potentially explosive situation became a constant topic of discussion. Local residents had signed petitions and sent people with a request that the Centre should be closed. There was serious consideration of closing the Youth Centre for a few months for a cooling off period. There were, however, those who believed that such a course of action would admit defeat for the ideals of an integrated Youth Club at Parchmore. In George Lovell's time at Parchmore similar problems had been experienced and experiments had been made in separating groups within the premises. This had had some success in the past and the idea was tested again and eventually the conclusion reached that the premises, both their nature within the building and their close proximity to houses, meant that we had to take a different course of action. The youth workers met, the Management Committee considered, the young people were talked with and the local residents involved. Eventually the decision was reached that the group of mainly white young people, who felt ownership from the past of the Centre, would go to another Youth Centre just a quarter of a mile away with two of the youth workers. This was not seen as creating segregated youth work but it had become obvious that the two major user groups of the Centre could not be worked with whilst the tensions of their meeting face to face every night of the week continued. It was hoped that programmes could be developed using two Centres so that joint activities could be created with an increasing frequency.

The neighbours around the Centre were invited to discuss the plans and made their suggestions. This process resulted in representatives of the local community joining the Management Committee.

Those who had resisted the two club idea eventually had to bow to its wisdom and the Centre settled into a period of creative work between the two groups as well as with the neighbouring community. Looking back we were only just becoming aware of the racism in the area and how this affected our ideal of a fully integrated club.

One incident brought home very forcibly to me the situation facing many of the black community in that area of London and, of course, many other areas. I was called one night to the local Police Station, when we had had a reasonable evening at the Youth Centre, and yet there was immediately the suspicion in my mind that something had gone wrong and the police had become involved. On arrival at the Police Station I was asked to confirm that I knew a person called Sylvan Eastmond who claimed to be employed at the Parchmore Centre as a full-time youth worker. He had been picked up on suspicion on his way home from the Centre. The policeman who had picked him up would not believe that a black person could be employed in a professional capacity. The struggle for freedom from prejudice was becoming part of the Parchmore story.

**Associated Youth Experiments**

The Parchmore Centre was established in a residential area of old Thornton Heath. Just a few hundred yards away an estate had been built called the Green Lane Estate. This was mainly Council housing with a large youth population which was unattracted by the youth work at the Parchmore Centre. Through discussions with the Borough Youth Officers and local people, an attempt eventually was made to establish a Centre on the Green Lane Estate.

The results are not amongst the most successful of the Parchmore Centre but they show how what had begun within the premises at Parchmore began to spill over into community activity throughout the whole Thornton Heath area.

We had also become aware, through the youth work, of the increasing problem of homelessness in that area of London. One evening Sylvan Eastmond had returned to the Centre because we had received reports on previous nights that lights had been seen and that people were breaking into the Centre. No evidence had ever been found but on this particular evening as Sylvan entered the building he became aware of noises in the Coffee-bar area and on some of the easy chair seating at the back of the Centre. He discovered various young people sleeping and on being awakened they said that there was nowhere else to go, it was either Parchmore or the streets. They had found a way in through a toilet window and were extremely careful how they used the premises and usually left no signs of their occupation. We discovered that they were but a few of the young people sleeping rough in shop doorways or in deserted premises in the area. It seemed to be a problem which was too large for us to tackle in any way. But a chance conversation led to the establishment of a project in South Norwood.

A large old house had been bought by South London Housing Association. It was surplus to their requirements at that particular time and was offered to the Parchmore Management Committee as a place where homeless young people could find shelter. It seemed too good an opportunity to miss and we agreed at Parchmore to manage the project. None of us had had any experience whatsoever in relation to homeless young people and we little knew what problems we were letting ourselves in for. The house was established and people offered a home and we sat back to await the grateful thanks of those whom we had helped. We were to find ourselves in situations which we could not have envisaged.

Rents were not paid and on one occasion the house was attacked and completely destroyed internally by a group of young people. At that point it would have been very easy to have said we could not go on with such a project. But it was maintained, the house gradually repaired and the project set on its feet again. We had learned that we had no right to expect people to be grateful to us or for those who had little idea of a home of their own to know how to treat a home established for them. It also showed in many ways our idealism and the belief that we could tackle anything. To be reminded of the fallacy of such an approach did not remove the idealism from the people at Parchmore. They had succeeded in many ways but there were also the failures. The failures were seen time and time again as an opportunity to reflect and to go on exploring the function of the Church in relation to its community.

**Becoming colleagues**

Making relationships was at the centre of much of the development during the years 1972–77. The Youth Centre Management Committee was reformed with representatives from the Local Council, the Social Services, members of the local community and the local churches. A deepening relationship with the local Authority resulted in the appointment of a minister as a youth training officer for the Borough of Croydon. Students became regular visitors to the Centre and there was deep involvement in training part-time youth workers through the local scheme and through the South East Regional Training Scheme based at Brunel University. Visits by students and courses held at Parchmore gave countless opportunities for new relationships and the telling of the Parchmore story.

The appointment of a community worker enlarged the friendship circle beyond all expectations. Good new relationships were made with the Social Services Department and we became regular contributors to social work training schemes in Croydon.

It was not only with Local Authority Social Services and Youth Services that relationships developed but major inroads into the life of the local community were made during those years. The creation of a club for retired people, which had become self-programming and firmly entrenched in the building, was used as the basis for the development of work within the community. It was found, through a survey of the area, that over six hundred people were receiving retirement pensions and living within a quarter of a mile radius around the Centre. The Borough of Croydon had been very slow in providing luncheon clubs but after considerable consultation such a club was created at Parchmore and met on two days a week. This was staffed by members of the church community and organized by the community worker and a voluntary worker who had come forward on hearing of the project. From this development the planning of the Good Neighbour Scheme within the area began to emerge. The establishment of Street Wardens for every street in the area who could maintain contact with elderly people, particularly those living alone, was begun. A newsheet was distributed regularly and the needs of lonely people referred back to the Centre. Help the Aged became involved and supported the project with gifts of money and the offering of their newspaper to be a means of communication. Many people became involved in this project, some of whom were members of the church at Parchmore and others who found themselves drawn into community development work.

A great deal about our ability to respond to people's needs was discovered in this process. One story will help to explore this. A church member called on a lady to discover her house occupied by over thirty cats. She had no fire, no warm clothes and spent all her money on feeding the animals. The house was in a dilapidated condition, it was dirty and it was obvious that the lady was suffering from malnutrition. If a bad winter was experienced then hypothermia was a distinct possibility. The visitor was a bachelor from the church in Parchmore. He had little experience either in his work life or in his church life of such a situation. He was embarrassed and wondered at his own adequacy in meeting any of the needs of the person of whom he was visiting. Over the months he established a relationship; the house was cleaned, clothes were found, electric fires provided, and both the visitor and the visited began to develop in ways that they thought quite impossible. Eventually the lady died and the visitor found himself in charge of all the arrangements for the funeral. He was there to say goodbye as he had been there to provide the last few years of the woman's life with warmth and human company.

The Good Neighbours Scheme developed into the possibility of a Drop-In Centre in the Parchmore premises. The story of the development is told later in the book but one exciting fun time was when consideration was given to where this Drop-In Centre should be. Parchmore premises were used all day and every day by a multitude of activities. There were Asian language groups, mothers groups, playgroups, luncheon clubs, youth organizations, play schemes, a work scheme for unemployed young people, and the thought of adding anything else to premises which were already full was quite a task. Where could we put it? Next to Parchmore was a house owned by the church and formerly the manse in which the caretaker lived and where the ground floor was used as offices for the minister and a small meeting room. Could this be utilized? Another dream began to emerge. At the rear of the house was a small garden enclosed by the church building, the house and the adjoining property. This had always been seen as waste space but could it be utilized to provide a Drop-In Centre for those who had been contacted through the work of the community worker? How could it be used? The idea of a portacabin began to be talked about. How on earth could it be established in a garden enclosed on all sides? It could never be said that Parchmore people were not imaginative and at one meeting called to explore the possibilities it was suggested that a helicopter could be engaged for a day and the portacabin dropped from the sky. This was not an idea that was immediately discarded, in fact it became a possibility and a goal to work towards. Eventually it proved to be impracticable and the Drop-In Centre was established on the ground floor of the caretaker's house.

The Parchmore story is one of development. There was increasing use of the building, large numbers of people from different sections of the community finding it a focal point of their life, and this, of course, resulted in many tensions between groups. The Community Council continued its work but increasingly found itself having an over-loaded agenda. The church community in some ways could have been forgiven for feeling frightened by so many people on the premises and engaged in the life of the community and Youth Centre. No doubt some people did feel threatened and thought that church life in many ways was taking second seat to the development of community activities. Others, however, saw what was happening as a direct result of their long years of planning, their group meetings with George Lovell, their dreams and their visions. There was a delight in the new opportunities created and a feeling of openness and outwardness which was exhibited in worship and in the committee structures of the church. Many of us were becoming increasingly aware of the role of the Christian community in developing and building community in its area. Parchmore was a centre to which people came, from which they went, and in which they worshipped and taught, planned, and ate together.

**Worship and the Church**

One of the features of life at Parchmore was vibrant Sunday morning worship. The early planning had led people towards what was called 'community worship' and the church was full of people of all ages and backgrounds, full of noise and activity. A visitor could be forgiven for believing that all was chaos and noise. This was the result of the community discovering ways not only to talk together but to worship together. Children were an important part of the development of community worship. A corner of the church was designated and furnished with bookshelves and books so that in the hymns, or indeed during the sermon, a stream of very young children would go to the shelves and find books and crayons and returning to their parents, hopefully, they would settle down so that the preacher could have what passed for silence for a few minutes to communicate with the congregation. No one objected for all were pleased to be together and no one seemed upset at noise or disturbance.

One Sunday the visiting preacher found the children too much to deal with and asked the parents to remove them. Indignant comments at the close of worship revealed just how much older members cared about the children as part of their community and possibly found more refreshment in worship in the activities of the children than in the words from the pulpit.

For the first time I discovered, as a leader of worship, a new freedom to explore and to experiment. A visitor from the South London Industrial Mission gave us some insights into new ways of exploring prayer and worship and preaching. It became a regular occurrence that papers appeared on the walls of the church where people could write in the names of the people about whom they were concerned and were asking for prayer. Favourite Bible passages were asked for by people during worship and the preacher used these passages to preach extempore and to explore the scriptures with the people. Hymn singing, special services and, of course, the usual run of church activities were maintained. There developed also a weekly Communion Service where a small number of people came together to break bread and to pray. This was the beginning in my ministry of the insight that no matter how active and busy a church community became, they still needed a heart where there was opportunity for silence and reflection and devotion. The new developments in worship helped me to discover the links between the non-directive approach employed in the work groups in the planning sessions with George Lovell and the development of our worship together. I discovered that preaching actually set up internal dialogues within people; that the sermon need not necessarily tell people exactly what to do and what to believe but that the method of Jesus was, in fact, to provide information and pictures, to tell stories and to enable people through those stories to discover for themselves the truths of the Kingdom of God.

The Christian community took seriously the charge to care for all. Through the Youth and Community Centre the building was open to all and through organizations the families of church people found also that Parchmore catered for much of their social life. The Axis Club which had developed during the early years of the project continued to meet the needs of middle-aged people. They and their friends met every Thursday to share in social activity; their children would meet in the Saturday Night Club, created for members of the Boys' Brigade and Girl Guides, and run by the husband of a community worker. The young people's group met on Sundays in the minister's home where I learnt a great deal about the youth culture of the day.

At times the different groups could be seen pulling in different directions. But whenever the need arose the whole community could respond together with compassion and commitment. One event which showed Parchmore at its best could have been a tragedy. One Sunday afternoon flames were seen through the windows of one of the church halls. Fire had broken out at the back of the stage and by the time the Fire Brigade arrived the hall was well ablaze. Flames leaped through the roof and people began to think that all the work of changing the building and its style was now going to be destroyed in an afternoon of fire. Fortunately the Fire Brigade managed to extinguish the fire and a few hours later we were viewing the premises damaged by water and blackened by fire. All groups and individuals started work. Much local labour was employed. Money raising activities, as well as the money received from the insurance, was all put into the pot and eventually the building was re-opened, redecorated and made new again. As someone mentioned, Thornton Heath without Parchmore had become unthinkable.

**Leaving**

By the time I had been at Parchmore for four years the activity and busyness had begun to lead us to a point of saying 'Is this the time to consolidate?' 'Is it the time to stop and take breath?' Certainly our ministry had reached a point where to leave was becoming the right option. With regret that decision was made by myself and my family, and yet in our own interests, and the Church's interest, it became apparent that the time was right. Parchmore had changed dramatically during George Lovell's time. Its building and its whole atmosphere and attitude had changed. During my years again change had been rapid. Large numbers of people were engaged and tiredness had come to be a constant companion. The processes at Parchmore had also changed. Whereas in George Lovell's time the whole church had gathered together to decide, now Parchmore was composed of the church and many other groups. The pattern of decision-making had changed. Decisions were now made in sub-groups and communication between them all was becoming more and more of a problem. One of the old-style level of consultations was held and it was fascinating to hear people talk of how they had changed and of how the church had changed through the years. People's conversations ranged over the years and comments of the history and of the present intermingled. Some of the statements are recorded below.

'Parchmore was now more open and receptive to the community as a whole and their needs.'

'People had become more tolerant but there were tensions because of the number of people using Parchmore and clashes of personality. Meetings and avenues had been established to help in these situations and the people now felt happier.'

One comment was 'It's a happier place for what we have done. I would rather have a place which has a bit of damage around than one which is a mausoleum like some beautiful churches and their premises'.

There was, however, a feeling that the church might not be as involved as it could be in the many community activities. But again there was a physical limit to what the church community could do. There was a sense of belonging and an atmosphere in which people felt happy. From within the church one could see enormous changes, but looking at these changes from outside some critical questions arose relating to the relationship between the church and the youth and community work. People commented on what they saw the minister doing and being. Questions were asked about whether that was the right role for a fully trained minister and whether the best use was being made of that resource. It could be seen that he carried an enormous burden, particularly as the work had developed, and in some people's estimation had fragmented. He very often was the only focus of unity for the whole of the community project. He was the one who was expected to know what was happening and to be able to communicate with all groups.

A comment from a church member is revealing, 'The exciting thing about this style of work is that in solving one problem you uncover another half a dozen, you don't just keep going you go faster, and faster, and faster'.

A member who had been in the project from the beginning made a very revealing comment, 'At the beginning we felt that open youth work could be a threat to us, and yet what is belonging to a Church? Is it a matter of signing a form or of belonging to a vibrant community? Since we stopped trying to make church members we have found many more people among us and willing to be part of us.'

'Parchmore has given me a great sense of vision and for those churches who are thinking that they may have to close, they can see what has happened here. It has not merely survived it is now a dynamic Christian witness.'

It must be stated quite clearly, however, that 'doing a Parchmore' should not be seen as any easy option. 'It is hard work. The process needs time. Results do not happen quickly and time must be allowed before results are assessed.'

The development in the Parchmore Road Methodist church could have affected relationships with other local churches but right from the beginning the youth work had at its base an Ecumenical Committee. Parchmore was never seen as empire building for as much work went into building relationships with other Christian communities as into the work within the Centre. Some had expected the church to lose its identity but that did not happen. In fact the church was strengthened and seemed to many to be more in keeping with its divine purpose. The community work was not being done at the expense of the church.

What did the new-found colleagues at Parchmore come to think of it? At a group held in 1977 there were representatives from Social Services, from the Youth Service and from the voluntary workers engaged in the Parchmore enterprise.

Speaking from the Social Service desk the Social Services Officer said 'Parchmore is an effective agency for care in the community'.

One of the voluntary workers engaged in the Neighbourhood Scheme said 'the going out from Parchmore is extremely important. Without it the community would not have developed its care system of Street Wardens'.

The Youth Service continued to use Parchmore as a training centre and its minister and youth worker on many training courses. It had become a central block in the building of a Youth Service in the Croydon area.

The time had now come for a change of ministry and in keeping with the established practice of involving as many as possible in any change and decision-making to be effected, groups were joined together in the Parchmore Church Youth and Community Centre to consider the nature of the ministry and the kind of minister that they would look for. Over the months documents were drawn up into a job specification and into a person profile. Some of the comments that came from the group indicated the nature of ministry as seen by the people at Parchmore.

'Parchmore needs a dedicated minister who really believes in the community development approach.'

'The pressures are enormous but I only believed in it because of the minister's belief in it.'

'It is necessary for people to know the leader will not opt out.' 'They have to be consistent in the way of working.'

'There is need for expertise and they need to direct people to expert advice where relevant.'

'Information is necessary which then leads to making good decisions.'

'The people at Parchmore would advise anyone to look carefully at the people who are promoting and thinking and ensure that they are likely to be consistent, skilled and committed over a long term.'

The resulting paper from all the negotiations pointed the way forward in terms of the full-time ordained ministry. It was important that there should be a collaborative style with the youth worker and the community worker and many voluntary workers. There should be a continuance of the methods of working. It would be wrong to go back to decision-making processes which did not include the people involved in the projects. It was also seen as necessary to invite someone who could be a focus of unity for the many different groups which appeared. Parchmore people saw this as the Bishop, the episcope in the true sense of the word. They had also come to believe that the time was right not to go on developing projects with the haste and speed of the past five years. They now looked for a minister with gifts in Christian worship and mission thinking. He was to be the expert in theology who would help the people to explore their faith in relation to the future development of the project. It was, of course, not only necessary for groups to be set up to write papers about the nature of ministry but actually to be involved in the decision-making process about who should come. People from the different groups were engaged from community work, from youth work, from the church, from the wider Borough of Croydon, from Social Services, all to be involved in meeting any prospective minister. The belief was that this was of vital importance in saying that the ministry which came should follow on the work of George Lovell and Garth Rogers for the past eleven years.

My own feelings on leaving Parchmore after five years of very busy, hectic, ministry, was one of intense gratitude of being part of a living, dynamic, Christian community. One which not only talked about doing things but got on with the action. I was grateful for the exciting, vibrant, worship and grateful for being able to reflect back and discover that through the years at Parchmore I had begun to move into new thinking in terms of the effectiveness of the Christian gospel. Community development is a process of helping people in their religious quest. It does this by working with people to discover how social and religious needs can be met. Together, members of a community work to develop appropriate ways of meeting their own needs.

# Part Three

## Seizing Opportunities for Mission and Unity

*– The Ministry of the Revd Peter Sharrocks 1977–89*

# 1. STEPPING STONES TO PARCHMORE

In 1971 the Methodist Church asked me to be the Churches' Youth Officer in Telford New Town. It was a new appointment made in response to the needs of young people and the desire of the churches to respond to them. No great strategy had been worked out. Not unusually for the Church, people were acting on an idea, and had managed to get enough money together to make a start. They hoped that I would be able to make the idea work! There was no real budget, and hardly any cash to spend on the work. The worker was the investment, and I was forced to start without anything to offer but myself, whatever skills and experience I had, and my commitment along with everyone else concerned for young people and the nurturing of community life.

I spent six very happy years in Telford, and I learned a great deal.

The churches had only just managed to scrape enough money together between them to pay my stipend, there was nothing budgeted for resources. When I went into the estates and introduced myself to the volunteer youth workers having a go at running clubs and coffee bars for the young people, I went empty handed. I had nothing to offer except my own willingness to work with them on the problems they were facing. This was in contrast to the statutory service which operated through a team of officers who went around with a programme of resources. The difference between having something to sell, and simply sharing the struggles of the people set the tone for my work, and became the basis of our relationships. I could not be their benefactor, only someone prepared to work with them on the things that mattered to them. I discovered real friendship and support as I worked with people who committed themselves to working together and with young people. I experienced a 'fellowship' at least equal to anything I have found in the church.

As we worked together, there was a growing unease between myself and the statutory youth service. The voluntary sector became more and more articulate as to its own needs and wants, and I was identified as someone who stimulated discontent. The fact was that discontent was there already, and what I and others did was become more skilled at making our point, and offering alternatives to the way the youth service was being delivered. I learned quickly that those in authority did not welcome criticism from 'below', and were suspicious of anyone who encouraged it other than themselves. They found it almost impossible to believe that ordinary people could think for themselves, so assumed any systematic criticism must be the work of a subversive professional!

Many people outside the Church found it difficult to understand why the churches' youth worker should be so concerned and involved with young people who did not go to church. When I offered my services to a local school, I had to convince them that I did not fit their preconceived notion of a youth minister. It was assumed that as a minister of religion I was only interested in my own agenda and in imposing my own ideas and beliefs on to people and situations. I had to demonstrate that I was genuinely interested in the young people themselves, and that I was particularly concerned about those at greatest risk or in severest need. In all of my relations with the secular professions I had to win their confidence before enjoying their co-operation. Once confidence had been won very positive and productive relations could develop.

One of the most important lessons I learned was never to assume that, or speak as though, compassion and sacrifice were the uniquely held gifts of Christian people. In working with the more needy end of the youth scene, I found myself alongside people who would never call themselves Christians who demonstrated passionate concern for others, and made many personal sacrifices in their commitment to the work we tried to do together. There was a small group of voluntary workers who for a couple of years met each fortnight to support one another, and learn how to do their youth work better. There were times in that group when we reached a rare level of spirituality as we struggled for the best way to help particular young people. I never knew the confidentiality of that group to be broken, and will never forget what we experienced as long as I live.

Whilst I was Telford Churches Youth Worker I had no churches to look after. The limited nature of my concern enabled me to see something of the impact the designs of politicians and planners have on people's lives. It was immensely frustrating to try to create a youth policy for Telford whilst political tensions bedevilled the relationship between the County Council and the Development Corporation. But things did change for the better and the Church did play a bigger part than it otherwise would have done because it chose to free a minister to concentrate on an issue.

I was commissioned to work with young people wherever they met, on the street, in clubs, schools, shopping centres. I had to learn new skills and I gained a new awareness. I had to learn how to study and explore communities, and to examine the needs of people in relation to their wider social setting. I became aware of the impact schools, the probation and social services and youth service had on young people. Not least I became acutely aware of how the quality of life available to young people is affected by politics and the economy, both factors over which they have very little, if any control.

My work inevitably brought me into working relationships with people in other professions, and I benefited enormously from my involvement with Staffordshire County Youth Service's training programme, and from the colleagueship of social workers, and community development workers. I learned new skills which were all to do with 'working with people'. They included group work, self-awareness, social profile and analysis, political awareness, and social action. We did not just talk about these things, but we lived them out, practising what we preached. I realized that I was re-working my theology, contributing the insights of the Christian faith, and sticking to the values of the gospel. So much of what I experienced echoed with the stories of Jesus' ministry; the welcome I received from the needy; the hostility of officialdom; the resilience of so many people whose lives had been fraught with hurt and disappointment.

I discovered a tremendous sense of adventure and fulfilment in working with all kinds of people to improve community life. We were striving together for change, exercising effective care on behalf of and with others. We were able to create new patterns of support for workers and for clients, and I had a deep sense of being with God with people in it all. The skills and insights I referred to above were the product of hard thinking, training and daily practice, and they seemed to me to be so fundamentally useful to Christian ministry.

I wondered whether I could return to a ministerial format which was primarily determined by, and devoted to, meeting the needs of church members. I had been introduced to a ministry which was community based, and aimed at the neediest. I had experienced the struggles and joys of changing things for the better in collaboration with others. I was committed to ways of working with people which I understood to be 'developmental' and which were greatly dependent upon exercising leadership in what was known as a Non-Directive way. I couldn't imagine many churches with the same commitments, priorities, or expectations of their minister, though perhaps I was being unkind or arrogant.

Garth Rogers had sought my services for Parchmore a couple of times. He had asked me to consider becoming youth worker and working with him, so I knew something about the place. When he invited me to consider becoming minister I was eager to explore the possibility. A couple of informal visits were arranged. I was introduced to the workers, and able to observe some of the work. I remember 'sitting in' on a day in Garth's ministry; listening to the day to day problems being discussed amongst the staff; attending a local secondary school for girls where Garth outlined the kind of work Parchmore was doing and the kind of place it was, as part of their religious studies programme. I remember roaming the streets, absorbing as much of the atmosphere as I could. I remember the liveliness of a church open for business. If my own ministry was to develop along the lines already begun in Telford, then this seemed like the next step to take. I wanted to be part of what was going on in a church which seemed to be so much involved in its local community. In the next twelve years I was to see the same kind of attraction in Parchmore capture the attention and commitment of so many other people.

The wheels of Methodism were set in motion as circuit officials arranged for a formal visit when I would be able to meet the circuit staff, and with my wife Barbara give some attention to the domestic details. A sequence of three interviews were arranged, to take place in one evening. These very clearly were the decisive part of the selection process.

One group was made up of church leaders both local and circuit, another was of people representing the church's youth and community commitments, and finally a group who I think were simply introduced to me as people who knew what Parchmore was about. By the end of the evening I knew that I had met with people who had a clear idea of what they were looking for, and were concerned to build upon what they felt they had already achieved. I was delighted to receive an invitation to succeed Garth Rogers.

## 2. ARRIVAL – INTO THE WHIRLWIND

I arrived at Parchmore after five years of rapid development under Garth Roger's leadership. New activities and commitments had been the order of the day, and a greater use of the premises by a greater variety of people than could have been imagined had simply 'happened'. There were those who thought that my coming would present an opportunity to stop awhile, catch the breath ...pause for thought. A nice idea and well-meant, but the work had a dynamic of its own. There were ideas floating around, projects in the pipeline, energies waiting to be deployed. It simply could not be stopped!

The desire for a pause was intended for my benefit, and to offer the church a chance to gain better control over what was happening. Rapid development was exciting, but there was anxiety about the pace of change threatening the unity of the church and the work. In the early days initiatives for new activities stemmed from the church members and were staffed by church volunteers, many of the new groups had arisen from community or professional sources outside of the immediate church, and were led by people other than church members. The more the ministry of the church extended into the community the more the community influenced the content of the work, and not everybody could see the connections between some of the new activities and the faith.

The tension was particularly acute in relation to the activities of a small Hindu group which met for fellowship and for worship. The question had been raised whether or not such an activity was 'a proper use of Methodist premises'?

There were more people using Parchmore than ever before, and there was a growing need for more office space to accommodate new members of staff. When would the developments slow down, or stop?

There was a fear that the church would lose its identity amidst the plethora of new projects.

It did not take long for me to realize that there was no stopping the process of development. Being increasingly aware of the needs of people in the neighbourhood, and concerned to respond positively wherever possible, was simply what it meant to be a missionary church. It was part of what Parchmore had become.

Without that 'spirit' Parchmore would become something else. On the other hand the questions that were being raised were important, and not to be ignored. If we became so active that we lost touch with our beliefs, or ventured into new areas of work without the consensus of the congregation we would lose an essential quality of being a place where 'community' is experienced. The nurture of Parchmore as a place of fellowship rather than dissension was just as important to the fulfilment of mission as the new activities we were getting into.

It became clear that if Parchmore was to continue to cohere we had to hold together as two sides of the same coin the key components of its life. The missionary activity in and with the community had to be pursued in ways that simultaneously nurtured and strengthened Parchmore's unity as a Church, Youth and Community Centre.

*Seizing Opportunities for Mission and Unity*
In effect it meant developing what we called a 'holistic outlook' in all that we did. It meant recognizing that an initiative in one area of work would have impact on other parts of the centre. We had to develop ways of working that prevented any abuse of other peoples' freedoms or ignored differences in opinion. In 'Telling Tales' some of the stories of development are told, and these illustrate the way we worked as we sought simultaneously to extend the work and build up the unity of the project. I am very conscious that I have left so much out but space does not permit the inclusion of everything. In the chapter on 'Managing' I try to describe some of the structures we adopted to help us fulfil our twofold goal of going all out for mission and unity. Finally I try to speak of leaving and letting go my involvement in a ministry with which I was totally involved and to which I was totally committed.

I am trying to write in story form, rather than a history of events, in the hope that the story will carry with it the sense of adventure and emotion that were so much part of the experience. I hope that readers may to some degree at least 'enter into it' and become part of it. I feel 'evangelical' about Parchmore's ministry in community. I want people to know about it because it is a model of church life that is so rare, and so alive with the struggles of love, and an ache for the Kingdom where barriers are ripped down, and the poor rejoice.

# 3. TELLING TALES

## WORKING WITH THE ELDERLY

### The Pop-In

One of the volunteers from the Good Neighbour Scheme was convinced that Thornton Heath needed a place for the elderly alone to drop into as well a visiting service in their own homes. She kept on about it to the community worker and when Help the Aged launched a national fund-raising scheme to establish Pop-Ins for the elderly nation-wide the idea was further explored.

A meeting took place between the volunteer, the community worker and the minister, and it was planned to gather more information, get in touch with Help the Aged to make a bid for financial support. By the time I arrived there had been a change of community worker, and Help the Aged had provisionally allocated a sum of money for a Pop-In scheme in Thornton Heath. The search was continuing for a suitable site.

At that time the ground floor of Parchmore House which used to be the manse and was situated next door to the centre was being used as an office for the community worker, and as a base for a youth unemployment project. The upstairs was the caretaker's flat. The ground floor was in great need of refurbishment, and the unemployment project was coming to an end. We wondered whether the ground floor could be converted into the Pop-In and some new accommodation for the community work base be developed alongside the youth worker's office at the youth centre entrance. It seemed desirable to all the full-time staff that they be seen to be working alongside one another, but there was resistance from some youth work staff and managers to the idea because they were anxious not to erode the youth work space of the centre.

A local builder estimated the cost of building alterations and improvements at £3,000 which was exactly the amount Help the Aged had offered us for a scheme, so the scheme was possible. Discussions were held with all the interested parties including the youth workers and management committee, and the Property Committee. After the consultation process a special Church Council was called to consider the idea. The whole matter was thoroughly discussed and the meeting decided unanimously to proceed with the scheme, authorizing the Property Committee to deal with the day-to-day management of the building side of things. I was greatly impressed by the Council's ability to examine the proposal and thrilled by their attitude towards the finances. They seemed to believe that if the need we were trying to meet was proven, and it was within our power to do something about it, then we should go ahead. They were quite convinced that the money would be found.

Once the go-ahead was given further meetings were held with the elderly of the church and the neighbourhood and a small fund-raising group was formed to raise the money needed to furnish the Pop-In. An open meeting was held for anyone who was interested in the Pop-In project, and ideas were shared as to the kind of place the elderly wanted it to be. Visits were arranged to other similar establishments. The workers were keen to ensure that the Pop-In was run as much as possible by the people who used it, and the involvement of likely users was encouraged from the beginning. The community worker worked with a small group of elderly activists throughout the period the building work was being done to establish the nature of the Pop-In, who it would be for, what provision it would make, how it would be staffed, etc. So well did these preparations go that the users were largely responsible for arranging their own opening day!

After the Pop-In had been open a few weeks the users started complaining about the church using the premises in the evenings! The sense of ownership of the project that had been engendered had gone too far and we had to explain our philosophy of sharing, and explain too the contribution the church had made in making the space available.

The opening is of course but another beginning. Over the years there is no doubt that the friendships that have been formed, and the care that has been given by people has been a lifesaver to many elderly and lonely people. One of the men who came into Parchmore's life at that time was a widower named Tom. It was years after the opening that he shared in worship at Parchmore and told us of the importance of the Pop-In to his regeneration as a Christian and a human being. His life had been shattered when his wife died, and until he became involved in the Pop-In project he had been almost a recluse. It was not just that he found a caring place, but that he found a real job of work to do in helping the project along. In spite of his own mobility difficulties he would go to help collect housebound people in the coach each week, befriend them and visit them. It was his greatest joy to be able to help others.

Tom was one of the many volunteers who day by day staffed the Pop-In, keeping it tidy, making the snacks, preparing lunches each Monday when a special lunch club was held for handicapped elderly, and generally being responsible for welcoming newcomers and keeping a watchful eye on those who came week by week. The skills of these volunteers are quite considerable. They are using in a community context the skills they have learned through life, at home and at work; skills of cooking, organizing and caring. The job of the community workers was to recruit and support them, and be available to give advice and help when it was needed.

Many other aspects of care for the elderly grew out of the initial project, a chiropodist visited regularly, there was a hard-of-hearing group through which people beginning to lose their hearing could get advice and hearing aids. The users of the Pop-In gave support to one another, and the kindness that was shown by the volunteer helpers to those in need was a joy to behold. There was also a considerable amount of forgiving love, too, as some very selfish and unhelpful users were 'borne with' over the years.

Our motto was not so much caring for the elderly as 'new life for the elderly'. From the beginning we wanted to give opportunities for service and recreational leisure to the elderly. In co-operation with Adult Education art classes were arranged and it was great to see eighty-year-olds picking up a paint brush after many years, or even for the first time.

They were discovering the joy of doing new things, of being creators in their old age. In conjunction with the local swimming baths a swimming club was started. One of the members of the Pop-In ran a dance session one afternoon a week. The Pop-In was also a part of the whole life of Parchmore and through it linked into the life of the town. They were not in danger of being forgotten. their skills were being used, and their wisdom was shared with professionals. A good example of this last point was the time when a group of newcomers arrived.

The newcomers all had severe learning difficulties, and had spent the previous fifty or so years in a mental institution. Unknown to us the programme of relocating these people into the community which we knew was coming had already begun. A private hostel had opened in Thornton Heath, and the Pop-In had been designated as an appropriate community provision. As a staff we were furious not to have been consulted, angry that the volunteers on duty had had no chance to prepare themselves for the challenge of this new situation, frustrated that we were not able to welcome this new group of people into the community as we would have liked.

We immediately contacted the Community Psychiatric Unit and the hospital concerned making our feelings known in no uncertain terms. There was a speedy response and a meeting arranged between Parchmore and the hospital staff responsible for the rehabilitation of patients. We expressed our deep concern at the assumptions being made about community resources. How did they know we were a suitable resource when they had not visited us?

Had they given thought to the preparation of communities to receive their patients? At this meeting we discovered that at least two other private hostels were shortly to open in the area and it had been assumed that they too would come to the Pop-In. At this first meeting an agenda for action was drawn up. It was clear that consultation was urgently required to:

- enable hospital staff to be more sensitive to the needs of the voluntary sector and community facilities;
- identify the extra support needed so that volunteer helpers in Pop-Ins and other organizations could respond helpfully to people with learning difficulties;
- assess just how many people could be accommodated within existing provision and how much new provision would be required;
- establish codes of conduct and links between the hospital service, hostel wardens and the voluntary sector;
- work with volunteers in the Pop-In to learn from them and help them cope with the new situation.

We arranged for the community psychiatric nurses to meet with the Pop-In volunteers. At this meeting the volunteers were able to share their own fears about their own ability and lack of confidence. They received helpful advice from the nurses and were able to express the difficulties they faced when confronted for the first time by a group of mentally handicapped people. An ongoing commitment was made between them, and the volunteers knew that whenever they became worried and concerned about the behavioural problems they encountered a visit by one of the psychiatric nurses could always be arranged. In the event the volunteers did amazingly well, and the Pop-In and Parchmore as a whole was enriched by the presence and contribution these newcomers were to make to our life.

## CONTINUING AND WIDENING CIRCLES OF CARE

During the period that I was minister at Parchmore work with the elderly continued to grow in scope. The lunch club, Pop-In and Good Neighbour Scheme, together with the contribution of the pastoral visitor were the backbone of the service. The numbers stayed fairly constant, but the degree of need became progressively more severe. As each year went by a greater proportion of the elderly were confused and feeble. Parchmore's philosophy was not out of sympathy with the general trend of keeping people in their own homes and neighbourhood setting for as long as possible, but the policy was putting increasing pressure upon community resources and the relatives of dependent elders. That pressure was felt directly by our own staff and volunteers. It was a concern to me and one which I shared frequently in policy consultations within the Borough.

Parchmore's reputation for good reliable service was confirmed when the local authority asked us to take over some rooms adjacent to two tower blocks of flats in which many elderly people were housed. The rooms were within ten minutes walking distance from Parchmore situated off the High Street. A small Good Neighbour Scheme had been set up by an organizer employed as part of the local social services team. On his retirement the social services department asked if we would take over responsibility for establishing a lunch club and community use of the rooms. A grant was available for a part-time worker to set this new piece of work up. The work is not exceptional in itself, but it does indicate the arrival of Parchmore as a reliable and trusted community resource, and also as an agency which would not simply provide a service but work for development in the community.

A lunch club was established at the *High Street* (as the base was called). Frozen meals were stored in a freezer and cooked on the spot. In addition to providing for the lunch, club meals were delivered by volunteers to the housebound elderly in the blocks of flats and this delivery service was Christened *Meals On Legs*! In due course the same service operated from the Pop-In to housebound people nearby. The strength of this method of meals delivery was that it was very local and an individual could only deliver a few meals, that in turn meant it was possible to establish better relationships between the customer and the deliverer.

The story told here is of continuing care and developmental work combining to provide a service that offers the elderly the support they need in a neighbourhood setting, and the opportunity to be carers and creators for as long as they are able. The story is one in which the initial involvement has led to new developments and a participation in the evolution of community care in the borough. The story does not parade the degree of commitment required of the workers, both paid and voluntary, without which these things of which I tell would simply not have happened. A flavour of the degree of care that is incidental to the work with elderly people can be gained by a brief recital of some of the day-to-day services rendered.

Day-by-day the staff will be attending to confused elderly people anxious about bills and new legislation affecting them. They will be checking-up on people who do not turn up for luncheon club for a few days to see if they are all right. They will help with arrangements for holidays, or with visits to relatives. They will act as go-betweens and contacts for anxious distant relatives. They will be keepers of keys for those who frequently lock themselves out of their homes. They will hear tales of woe and be complained about and at. They will keep an eye on all of their clients for any tell-tale sign of deterioration and take appropriate action. They will arrange for hospital visits and spiritual counsel. And inasmuch as they have done it to the least of our sisters and brethren, they will have done it unto the one who is servant of all.

**The Playgroup**

The Playgroup was a well-run, efficient rather than friendly outfit, with parent participation kept to a minimum. In other words not at all typical of a community development project. When I asked for a copy of the constitution I received a short letter back which informed me that the Playgroup had managed very well without one for a number of years – thank you very much! I decided to leave things as they were for the time being.

Eventually the leader retired and was succeeded by one of the church stewards who, though influenced by her predecessor, was of a different disposition and after receiving training through the Playgroup Association wanted to promote more parent participation. At around the same time there was something of a financial crisis, and it came to the attention of the playgroup staff that as things stood (i.e. without a constitution) they were liable to be held personally responsible for the fortunes and misfortunes of the Playgroup. They became very interested in getting a constitution!

The new leader asked for advice from Diana Morrison the community worker, and myself, so having been held at bay for years, we were now invited in to help with the reformation of the Playgroup. There followed some fairly detailed and systematic work with the staff, and the few parents who were used as helpers in the Playgroup.

The staff were a mixture of church and non-church women, and at first there was strong resistance by the non-churchers to the idea that the Playgroup be an integral part of Parchmore. They were highly suspicious that this was a take-over bid by the church. They argued that the Playgroup should be independent and simply rent the premises. The church members were less than happy with this suggestion. The community worker and I explained the supportive nature of the church's involvement, and the beliefs and ideas that were behind the desire to ensure that the people who used Parchmore were part of the church and centre as a whole, with rights and privileges which could be enshrined in a constitution. The options were tested, tried and clarified, and eventually the suspicions were overcome and work began on formulating a constitution which embodied a positive relationship between the

Church Council, and the Playgroup, and incorporated the involvement of the community-work staff.

The new constitution also reflected the emphasis of the Playgroup Association, giving a much larger role to the parents as managers. The staff were convinced that no parents would get involved, but after a struggle, enough were drafted-in to satisfy the requirements of the constitution, and work with them began. At first all attention was focused on the immediate needs of the Playgroup; a rota for parental involvement was drawn up, fund-raising activities began. Ideas and responsibilities were shared.

Parents also began to make plans to meet their own needs, arranging social evenings where conversation ranged far-and-wide and new ideas were tossed about. They started a coffee morning to cultivate interest among the parents who so far were resilient in resisting any more contact than dropping their children off and picking them up. The activist mums found it very hard to suppress their anger and disappointment that they only won the participation of the few. We tried to encourage them, and help them to rejoice in what they were achieving rather than getting downhearted about the things that did not go as well as they would have liked.

One of the joys of all this was the improvement in relations between all parties involved. The Church Council had to wrestle with its responsibilities as the overall management group, the staff of the centre and the staff of the Playgroup and the parents learned to work with each other, and forged friendly relationships. The parents began to play a more significant role in the life of the centre, and some of them began to bring their children to church on Sunday mornings.

It was a concentrated piece of development work with one section of the centre, which led to change for the better in so many ways.

**Family Groups**

When I arrived in 1976 the European Community was sponsoring various programmes of community action on a number of fronts. One of these initiatives was to select two areas in Britain for a project whose purpose was to establish a support–network for families under stress in which children were perceived to be at risk.

Croydon was one of the local authority areas chosen, and Thornton Heath in particular. Parchmore was approached as a possible venue, and preliminary discussions were held between the national project workers, the local authority representatives, and Parchmore through its minister and community worker.

The outcome from these discussions was the formation of three Family Groups in the Thornton Heath area, one based at Parchmore itself. Each of the groups was to have a paid support worker, and child attendant. The funding was from European Community sources, and paid to the individual workers through Croydon's Adult Education system. The Parchmore Community worker became a support worker to the project, which meant keeping in touch with the three groups through their workers, visiting the groups occasionally, and organizing regular meetings for all the workers periodically so that they could give one-another mutual support and encouragement.

The minister as Team Leader at Parchmore acted as a consultant to the community worker, and occasionally to the group workers. Whenever there were meetings between the various sponsors, that is the national project workers and the Adult Education Officers, the minister would work alongside the community worker as one of Parchmore's representatives. Invariably our role would be to enable the Family Group workers to get their views and feelings across to those who at that stage were acting as managers to the project.

The process of establishing Family Groups was fraught with all the difficulties of inter-disciplinary, and multi-agency collaboration. Adult Education regulations required that a certain number of parents had to be involved in a group to justify funding; a regulation designed for basket-making or pottery, rather than for group support for people under stress! Getting a sufficient understanding of what the nature of the groups was, and how to appreciate their worth was not easy either.

Eventually the European funds were to cease and there were anxious times as alternative sources of money were found. A transition to local management had to be negotiated, training courses for new workers initiated, and equal opportunities thinking and practice to be integrated into working practices.

The tenacity and conviction about the worth of what was being done by those who were actually doing the work with the beleaguered parents was reflected in the resilience of Parchmore's community worker. She became Chairperson of the Management Committee, and in due course the Family Groups extended throughout the Borough.

How does one measure the effectiveness of this piece of work? Who knows what benefits have been received by the parents and children? How do we know that the effort has been worth it? We are often in the realms of testimony, as over the years those who have been part of a group have bumped into the workers and expressed their gratitude. But there is also the evidence of people getting themselves 'sorted out'. Getting the skills to manage their domestic lives better through the programmes of the Family groups themselves, which are tailor-made to the needs of the group members. It can be measured in the growing self-confidence of individuals as they share their favourite cooking dishes with other members in the group, or help one another out in all kinds of ways. It can be measured in the numerous calls for help in a crisis, when because of the group's existence, there is somebody to reach out to, and ask help from.

It is also worth noting another development which took place as a direct result of the Family Groups. It was important to find outlets for group members. They were not after-all expected to stay in a Family Group for ever! Some of the mums came up with the idea of forming a badminton club. They wanted to meet in the mornings as this suited their domestic circumstances best. They also wanted to have instruction. It was discovered that all the provision of a recreational nature took place in the evenings, and this was of no use to them. 'We have to feed our husbands, put the baby to bed. There's no way we can get out at that time.'

Meetings were held between Adult Education Officers and the mums, and Parchmore workers. A morning badminton class was started, with Parchmore recruiting crèche assistants to help the parents look after the children, and providing accommodation, and Adult Education providing tutors.

This was the first of many activities in Parchmore which were run for parents of young children, and the idea has spread beyond Parchmore into other parts of the Borough.

A few weeks before I was to take up the appointment at Parchmore the *Methodist Recorder* ran a full-page article about a project for homeless young people which had just begun. The article anticipated all kinds of possibilities for extending provision across south London. I began to wonder what I was getting myself into!

I inherited one dilapidated house, which was occupied by six young people, a resident warden, an alsatian dog left behind by the previous youth worker who had lived-in for a period to weather the storm of a crisis, and a small group of people who acted as 'day to day' managers of the project.

However crack-pot it seemed, this was the only provision in Croydon for young people who were homeless and relatively destitute. Both the youth worker and the community worker were on the small managerial group, with a local schools counsellor, a senior social worker, an architect working in the special housing projects field, and myself. We met every month with the warden, and sometimes with some of the residents too. In these meetings we sought to identify the needs of the residents, resolve some of the behaviour problems that arose between them, and find ways of getting the rent from them!

There were all kinds of problems associated with the building; getting repairs done, keeping the garden reasonably tidy, and the neighbours 'happy'. The property was owned by the Greater London Council, and managed for them by a South London Family Housing Association, who were sympathetic to the problem we were trying to deal with, and remarkably uncomplaining landlords.

Each young person had his or her own room, and they shared bathroom, toilet, and kitchen. The rooms varied in quality, because each occupant had responsibility for their own room. If they wanted to redecorate, we would help with materials. If they lived in a mess, we did not clear up for them! If they messed up the communal areas there would be trouble between residents, and the warden got them to sort things out by arranging rotas. These would work for no more than a week or two unless there happened to be a resident capable of holding the arrangements together.

In spite of all the shortcomings of the provision, the demand for its use was ever increasing. Desperate social workers would ring and ring again to see if we had a vacancy for their clients, as would the agencies dealing with homeless young people in central London. The project was taking more and more of Parchmore's worker's time as they sought to keep records of enquiries, manage the property, and respond to the needs of, and sort out the disputes between, residents.

We were dissatisfied with the service we were able to offer, and accommodation we were able to provide, and yet there was clearly a desperate need which nobody else was responding to.

After three years surviving, the project was under pressure to vacate the premises by Croydon Borough who wished to clear the site to make way for an extension to the adjacent Shaftesbury Housing residential home for the elderly. Those of us who were involved in the project were tiring, and in need of a way out that would lead to better provision for homeless young people. I had had enough of being called out in the middle of the night to help solve the disputes of residents, or assure the police that the person they had 'picked up' really did live at 22, South Norwood Hill!

The Croydon Guild of Voluntary Organizations initiated a Special Housing Needs group, and because of our involvement through the hostel Parchmore was involved. In its early stages the group established its priorities, and the needs of young people were highlighted. We were able to form a new group of people who were to commit themselves to the creation of new housing project for homeless young people. It was no longer a Parchmore group, but I became its chairperson, and the experience that had been gained over the years was invaluable as we worked together. The group which emerged could best be described as a consortium of interested parties. They included Nightwatch, (an organization which had a hostel for adults, and organized the soup run to the homeless in Croydon), the local CHAR, the Croydon Churches Housing Association, Croydon YMCA, and YWCA, the Social Services, and the Probation Service.

This group formed itself into the Croydon Association for Young Single Homeless (CAYSH), and worked unceasingly for two years to get the new project off the ground. This meant establishing the case for the project by getting statistics together, and writing proposals for action. Formulating a constitution and getting charitable status. Getting the support of the local authority housing committee so that Urban Aid could be applied for, making application for funding from Urban Aid, and the Home Office.

Once the funding had been secured, a property was found by Croydon Churches Housing Association and the hostel designed, and built to provide an intake unit and two shared flats, plus office accommodation. Interviews for the four members of staff took place and appointments made. It was not perfect, these things never are, but it was a gigantic step forward from those early days in a short-life property, and a hand to mouth existence.

Young people who were homeless or in housing difficulty in Croydon now had a service which offered them advice and worked with them to solve their housing problem. This might mean helping them to resolve differences with parents, to finding a place to 'cool down' after a domestic row, it might mean offering accommodation within CAYSH properties, or finding them accommodation elsewhere, in other hostels, or in bed and breakfast accommodation. It would mean helping to process claim forms for various allowances and benefits.

It is important to give some idea of time scale in all of this.

- Parchmore opened their hostel in 1976.
- CAYSH was formed in May 1980.
- The CAYSH hostel was opened in September 1983.
- Additional units of housing were opened in July and November 1984.

One of the additional units was in fact a replacement for the original Parchmore hostel. When the local authority sought to get us to move out from 22, South Norwood Hill, we argued that closure would force the residents on to the street, and make them homeless, and therefore the council was bound to offer alternative accommodation, which they did.

As CAYSH developed, it became more and more evident that the situation of young single homeless people was getting worse rather that better. Legislation affecting the entitlement of young people to housing benefits, and the pernicious legislation which forced them to move from place to place in search of work and accommodation had to be opposed. Campaigning for a better deal for the young homeless, and educating all sections of the community about such matters has become part and parcel of CAYSH's work.

The work goes on.

## BLACK AND WHITE TOGETHER

Brixton is four miles north of Thornton Heath, close enough to feel the reverberations of the disturbances that took place there in 1981. It felt very near. The young people were buoyed up by the drama and National Front activity was busier than usual. The youth club could be tense especially when older strangers appeared or the police cruised visibly by. Black youths complained about their young sisters and brothers being harassed on their way to and from school by skinheads. Black parents were worried about the same thing. In spite of the signs and our forebodings we were still not ready for the shock and hurt of what was to happen on June 1st.

There were more people than usual at club that night, and numbers gathered outside, but there was no trouble at the club itself, just a tension in the air. Unknown to us, Parchmore had been chosen as the meeting point where black young people were to gather before going into the High Street to do damage to the pub where a number of National Front whites met, and to inflict injury upon them. After the club had closed a rush to the High Street began, and the assault on the pub took place. It was a frenzied event, windows were broken, some injuries inflicted but that was not to be the worst of it.

When the police arrived the youths scattered, and one group of fifteen or so in a state of hysteria dashed around the side streets. For reasons never to be found out, they set upon a young man whose name I will never forget and whom I never met, Terry May. He had had nothing to do with the previous events of that night, and was an admirer of Bob Marley who sung the cause of black liberation. Terry was stabbed and he died within minutes.

The next day Thornton Heath was headline news, and Parchmore was soon singled out for particular attention. Extremists from right and left, black and white, threatened to burn the premises down or attack the workers. We were embroiled in a whirlwind of police activity and media pressure. We were identified as the friends of black young people in the area, and wished to stand with them still whilst condemning the violence. We wanted to show sympathy to the bereaved and to offer support to the young people we worked with. It was a baptism of fire, and the end of soft pedalling on the race issue.

For years Parchmore had sought to provide space in the community for young people to meet, and to provide a structure in which they could safely enjoy themselves. For years we had hoped that being a place of hospitality to so many different nationalities would help the transition to a peaceful multi-racial community. In the period following June 1st it felt as though we had been naïve, and had failed to respond in a sufficiently bold way to deal with prejudice and the disadvantage of being black.

A special murder squad was sent in, special in that they had received training for work in racially sensitive situations. Police vans with riot shield visors over the windscreens toured the streets night and day. Dawn raids on black people's homes were frequent as suspects were rounded up and information was sought. We were working with the police and also with black young people to ensure that there was no escalation of tension or violence. The police urged us to 'carry on as normal'. It was not easy to do.

June 1st was the Monday before Whit Sunday, the Feast of Pentecost, and arrangements had been made for the church to have a picnic in a Croydon park after the morning worship. It was the last thing I felt like, but a lay leader persuaded me not to call it off, and he was right. It was a very special Pentecost. The worship area is upstairs – an upper room. The police were still keeping an eye on the building just in case one of the lunatic threats should materialize. Worship crackled with the presence of God as he assured us of his power and love, and gave us strength in our solidarity. After worship we went to the park, and as a multi-racial church demonstrated that enmity between races would never be the last word as we ate, played and prayed together. In the evening ninety people attended the evening service when normally twenty-five would have been a good score, and we talked together and shared together about the previous week's events.

The tragedy of June 1st was to have a significant impact upon our work in the community and our life together.

**Thornton Heath Community Forum**

In partnership with the Croydon Guild of Voluntary Organizations a Thornton Heath Community Forum was initiated. This was a coming together of local residents, local churches, representatives of black and Asian groups in the area, the police, youth and community workers and social workers. Now all the hospitality that had been offered over the years was to pay off. Parchmore was uniquely placed to play host, and to initiate such a venture in peace-making, and to bring the many different factions together in what was then a torn, hurt and fearful community.

In the Forum the truth was pursued and affirmed in an attempt to counter the many rumours that surface in situations of neighbourhood tension. Some tough talking took place about the policing of the area and efforts were made to influence police training, and to improve the effectiveness of community policing. There was face to face dialogue with senior management of the local press, in an attempt to identify how they could make a more positive contribution to racial harmony, and to make specific criticisms where necessary. Local Government officers attended the Forum for discussion about their policies for education and youth work as it affected black young people, and the multi-racial community.

One of the more dramatic events during this period was the emergence of a Black Action Group, which amongst other things announced that it had formed a corps of vigilantes to 'police' the streets of Thornton Heath and protect the interests of black people. The Forum called an open meeting at Parchmore so that the local community could have its say on the matter. During this very lively and intense meeting it became very clear that the vigilantes were not wanted, and that the Black Action Group did not speak for local people. The local people wanted better, non-racist policing. This meeting was noted for the vigorous participation of youths and adults together.

The Forum met for two and a half years, by which time the crisis was over. It sought to widen its brief and look collectively at other community-wide issues. It failed to attract sufficient support from local residents, though the professional workers involved still met. It came to an end. But as a model for helping a community deal with a crisis situation, get its voice heard and take initiatives of its own it certainly worked well. And the relationships that grew as this various group of people met together were to last for a long time, and the things we learned will last for ever. I shall always treasure the occasion when we discussed 'commitment to the community' from the perspective of the Hindu, Moslem and Christian faiths. Networks between the various ethnic groups, the Guild of Voluntary Organizations, and Parchmore itself were significantly improved, and these together with our own much heightened awareness of racial issues paved the way for discussions within our own organizations about equal opportunities, and combating racism generally in the town.

**Facing Up to Our Own Racism in the Church**

The violence which erupted in Thornton Heath, and Parchmore's connections with it was at first a shock and deep disappointment, that all the work we had done over the years could not prevent such a thing happening. On reflection it was also an awakening, and like the first Pentecost, became the start of much new life, new consciousness, new programmes of work, and it began with repentance. An event took place in our life which revealed to us much that previously we had not seen. Black people were provoked to say things about their experience and we were ready to listen. We heard first-hand from members of our own congregation about the cold shoulder many had got when first they came to England and sought the fellowship of the church. We heard about the people who lived next door who threw their rubbish into the garden of their new black neighbours. We heard about the pain of black office workers who smiled in the face of middle-class racist remarks veiled in humour, the kind which is justified with phrases like, 'Oh they don't mind, they laugh as well.' We heard that after the laughter one of our most beloved members would slip away to the toilet and weep. We heard about the people who walk their dogs round the quiet suburban streets and always make sure their dogs pause to defecate at the gate of the black family. We heard about young people frequently being picked up by the police, and how black youth workers returning home at night were often stopped and searched. The white youth workers never were. As we walked the streets of tension, constantly looking over our shoulder, I vividly remember a black youth saying to me, 'That's how it always is with us. Now you know!'

### Affirming Black People and Black Cultures

The revelations described above did not tumble out in orderly fashion. But they were released in various settings within the fellowship of the church acting on a proposition by its black members at the Annual Church and Centre Meeting to examine black issues in its own church life. From that moment the issue of race relations was openly on the agenda, and we sought to affirm and confirm our commitment to multi-racial living and facilitate black participation.

All the committees sought to include black representation; the mainstream events of church life were reviewed in the light of a renewed awareness of the need to affirm our joy at our multi-racial nature, and our anticipation of a fresh contribution from people of other lands and cultures. Since the conversion of Parchmore into a church, youth and community centre, our pride had been very much in the work that we did, and our identity dominated by our being a community development project. We made much of the history of that development, now we were to recognize that our identity was far richer than that. Our history was the history of a membership drawn from the continents of the world, and in particular from Africa and the Caribbean. We needed to affirm their history too, and receive their insight and personalities. We had to cease carrying on as though we were still a white European congregation, to do so was tantamount to denying the existence of our growing new membership, the people God was giving to us, the people who were our neighbours.

### Farewell to the Traditional Harvest Supper

The Harvest Celebrations included a harvest supper cooked by various groups in turn. All the adult groups were mostly if not entirely white. The food provided always European. The World Service and Mission Committee recommended that the supper be organized to include food from four continents, Africa, the Caribbean, Asia and Europe. In the event America was also included, so there were five continents. It was argued by some that such an event was more suitable for One World Week, but this was resisted and we began to learn that the acceptance of black people meant altering our normal life, not bolting on additional bits. It meant change in everybody and everything to do with our life together, and we began with the Harvest Supper.

The families from Africa and the Caribbean responded magnificently, and our Asian family produced a table on their own, using the resources of their extended family to provide almost enough for everyone to have a taste of their cuisine. It was a very joyful event. I believe it was also a liberating event. From this point onwards there began a surge of participation by black people in the life of the church. More became members of the church committees, took responsibilities in leadership at every level, and took part in social events.

**Studying Racism in Fellowship**

The regular Church Fellowship which met fortnightly used a course of study devised by the Evangelical Alliance for Urban Mission in which the history of racism and its philosophical roots were studied, and the biblical basis for an anti-racist stance based on equality and justice was explored. During this a detailed examination of Immigration Policies was made, and I realized that pulpit rhetoric about a government's racist policies convinces very few people. Accusations of that sort have to be backed up by hard work, and cogent argument to demonstrate the meaning of what has been said. Mouths dropped open as the history of British immigration policy was charted and the ever closing door to black and Asian people was contrasted with an ever opening door to white people, giving away the lie of the numbers game. British immigration and nationality law has not been about keeping people out, but keeping black people out.

**Challenging Racist Language in Church and Centre**

We had experienced something of the pain and the destructiveness of the evil that racism is. It became more and more important to those who worked at Parchmore that whenever racist remarks were made they should be challenged, and countered with questions or information which would help people think more accurately and positively about the multi-racial community in which we were all now living.

When jobs are scarce and housing is in short supply it is all too easy for the indigenous population to blame those whose origins were not British. The most obvious of these were the black and Asian people. It can get boring but I tried to remind people of what they knew but insisted on disregarding, that loss of jobs was about the economy, and the shortage of housing was due to failures in housing policy; that the black and Asian people were connected with us by right because there had been something called the British Empire; and that the transition to a multi-racial society was initiated by a British Government to help us solve our own domestic economic development following the second world war. And anyway there was a great deal of potential in a multi-racial society, and to my way of thinking it was not a 'bad' thing but a 'good' thing.

When we were confronted by negative attitudes to multi-racial living we always tried to help people to a more positive attitude by getting them to examine their own experience of black people, and by testifying to any 'good stories' of our own. I also tried to get people to face the fact that history was not going to be put into reverse. We had to face the question of what kind of society we wanted to live in, a peaceful harmonious one, or a bitter, divided and potentially violent one. Christians had a vision of corporate life, and it could only materialize if we managed to love one another, and that meant increasing our understanding and appreciation of those who were different from ourselves. It also meant learning to face up to our own past, and forgiving one another and ourselves.

Over the years it was encouraging to see how the church learned to speak freely about black and white issues, and how they learned to use the language with some comfort. In a very real sense black became beautiful so we lost any fear of using the word to describe others. I can only guess that some of the negative connotations of blackness had dropped away because of the very positive experience we had of fellowship in an increasingly multi-racial church. As a church and centre we became more and more proud of our multi-racial nature.

The language of worship also altered. I became aware that so many prayers are written as though the congregation is all of one nation, or of singular religious tradition. The language of worship needed translating to affirm the plural nature of the situation we were in. Events affecting the islands of the Caribbean, and the continents of Africa and Asia were matters of shared concern, action and intercessory prayer. Barrels of aid in response to hurricanes, gifts of money and kind to assist the village congregations of our members' indigenous churches. Not least preaching that faced up to the evils of racism and injustice and called for repentance and renewal. The rhythms of Reggae and the tradition of Black spiritual music were incorporated, and influenced my own writing of songs for worship. We discovered that as we looked at our life from a plural perspective new ways of doing things presented themselves, and new energies were released.

**Black Leadership**

In the church life as I have mentioned there was a surge of black participation in leadership, but this was not matched in the community work. In part that is due to the fact that we were not able to find or use opportunities to employ black workers. In fact over the twelve years of my ministry there were only three vacancies which occurred. In two of them it was a matter of 'making up' people who had already proved themselves. One as a part-time worker, and the other as someone placed with us for work experience. The third vacancy was for an office worker and receptionist. We did deliberately set out to employ a black worker, and succeeded in doing so, but it did not work out for either party. Either it was not the right job for her, or else we did not work hard enough at resolving the difficulties we each experienced. I think most of them centred round the great difference between working in a controlled office environment, and a short staffed voluntary organization where no matter how carefully one works out job descriptions, workers have to be willing to cover for one another frequently, and generally have the combination of initiative ability and commitment to 'muck in'.

I have no doubt that if we had been more determined, maybe we could have done better in this department, and it would have been helpful to discover the effects on us as a staff team, and those who used the centre. But one has to put that loss alongside the productiveness of an enduring staff team .

In youth work, we simply failed to attract black applicants to the post of full-time worker in spite of making every attempt to do so. On reflection maybe we should have kept trying rather than appointing the best of those who applied. But to do that meant facing increased responsibilities and pressure upon those 'holding the fort', not least the minister. It would also mean we would have lost the contributions we received from the white workers who knew what they were taking on, and chose to work in a black environment.

Nearly all of the groups which meet at Parchmore have their own leadership, and a measure of independence. The degrees by which these came to be more sensitive and less racist varied. The Playgroup, which was very multi-racial was fairly quick to employ other than white staff, but took a long time to produce its publicity and information in any other language than English. The centre-wide events gave an opportunity to bring people from different groups and nationalities together either in celebration or simply to work together for common cause.

### The Wider Scene

I have indicated that Croydon did not exactly relish its multi-racial character, and was slow to examine itself, its practices and services in the light of equal opportunities legislation. Both during the disturbances of 1981 and afterwards Parchmore staff and a number of its lay people were regularly involved in efforts to raise awareness, and improve race relations in the town's life.

- We participated in a programme of induction for new police officers.
- We participated in equal opportunities review for Croydon Guild of Voluntary Organizations, and the Croydon Youth Service.
- We helped to initiate a detached youth work project in the north of the borough.
- We visited other churches in the borough to share our experience.

### The Multi-Faith Dimension

When I first arrived at Parchmore there was an item on the church council agenda, which looked like my first 'hot potato'. It was a question to be considered, and had to do with the whether it was right for Methodists to allow worship by people of another faith on their premises. The question was not an academic one. The initial hospitality offered to Ugandan and Kenya Asians had continued. What began as a small meeting of elderly men had extended to a small family act of worship on Saturday afternoons. In addition there were regular bookings of the Youth Centre as a venue for Hindu weddings, or for special family occasions which were usually accompanied by prayers.

When this question was raised again it was agreed that it was not a matter for hasty decision-making, and that it raised profound questions about our own faith, our own attitudes to people different from ourselves, and what relationship our faith requires us to have with people of other faiths. It was agreed to spend a year giving ourselves time to study the issues. I do not think we did this particularly well, but certainly we came to a decision at the end of the process, in which we declared that our first priority in the process of developing relationships was to offer hospitality, and this should be continued.

It became evident that the more people associated with good people of other faiths, the less certain they were about taking a 'superior attitude'. One or two members confessed that the devotion of some of the people they had come to know through the life of the centre put them to shame. A talk given by Revd Edward Rogers on the matter of multi-faith relations left us in no doubt that we had much to learn, and there would be much that we would never altogether understand. It was not a disgrace to confess ignorance, but to acknowledge how much we had to learn again left room for charitable judgments.

At the end of the day, I think we wanted to do what would be most helpful in promoting harmonious relations in the centre and the community. It is a fact that once the church had set out to be part of the community, and declared as one of its purposes the encouragement of a community life built around the values and hopes of the gospel, it is not easy to start excluding people from the centre which claims to be working with and for the whole community, regardless of race, colour, class, wealth or religion. Once one understands that people of other faiths integrate their devotion and social life so completely it becomes impossible to make distinctions between people on grounds of their beliefs. Were we to be happy to accept atheists playing badminton, but to exclude Hindu's saying their prayers?

The question was to be reconsidered a few years later when the Methodist Conference was to examine the legitimacy of the use of Methodist premises by people of other faiths in respect of charity law. At that time, the Church Council reaffirmed its commitment to 'hospitality', but felt obliged to curtail the more blatant contraventions of the law by ceasing to be a venue for large gatherings like weddings and cultural celebrations. Even so there was a preference for the charity law to be changed. It seems there was a feeling that what we were doing at Parchmore in building up a multi-racial, and multi-faith community was somehow consistent with Christian ministry and mission.

At the end of my time at Parchmore, the question was raised again, this time by a number of members in the church, who had found stimulation in their own religious experience through more evangelical groups, and charismatic fellowships. They were not against people of other faiths, nor against their being offered hospitality on the premises, but they felt very strongly that the one remaining worship group (the small family worship on Saturday afternoon) should no longer continue.

There was a lengthy discussion in the Church Council, and it looked as though the small worship group would have to end. Just before a vote was to be taken I felt a distinct unease in the meeting. I asked if they were sure that this is what they wanted to do. Black people in particular began to express themselves, and were very much against excluding this group.

I can remember one woman asking, who would be next to be excluded.

Another asking, if it was not God that these people were worshipping, who was it? I was acutely aware that we were hearing the voice of the voiceless. People who knew what it was like to be rejected, and looked down on were speaking up for a group in the life of the centre whose faith they did not share but whose experience in life they understood only too well. The vote was taken, and was in favour of the small worship group continuing.

The questions will linger on. The issues of race and faith and Christian witness still need much exploration and nerve. What this final discussion revealed was how passionately, and sincerely, different views can be held, and how inter-related are the issues of faith, race, and mission in a plural society.

When I went to Parchmore it had a membership of about 150, when I left it had a membership of about 150, so there is no story of phenomenal growth in terms of people joining the church. On the other hand the church has managed to maintain its numbers at a time when most other mainstream Christian congregations in the area have been going through a period of steady decline. But ought we to get into such crude estimates of success or failure as membership figures? After all an ex-president of the Methodist Church once said that if the Church really took the gospel seriously in word and deed the membership might well be halved!

I am of course biased and eager to advocate the kind of church that Parchmore has become with all my heart, and to try and do justice to the struggles and sacrifices that have been made. It is not of course perfect, and there are no guarantees about its future, but in some important respects I believe the people have made some significant steps in translating gospel imperatives into positive action.

All ministers must cope with the ghosts of their predecessors, and it was no less the case with me. George Lovell and Garth Rogers had left their mark in both church and community, and their predecessors also lived on in the memory of the people. This book focuses on three ministries which were quite deliberately related to each other by a strategy and purpose worked out by the church, and this has meant a complementary and sustained period of development in its life and work.

In my own case great care was taken to ensure that my leadership would be exercised in ways that encouraged people to share in the thinking, planning and decision-making. They understood and had experienced what non-directive leadership meant and wanted to keep it! There was a job description which had been worked out by the church leaders with Garth's encouragement and help. It is a good indicator of where they were in their thinking about the centre on my arrival in 1977.

This document had a very liberating effect because I did not have to argue for or defend the time I was to spend being involved in the community, making a contribution to various groups, and working with others in response to human need. Those things were specified as part of my job. It also made it clear that the ministry belonged to the whole people of God, it was not something done by 'the minister'.

Most importantly it identified what was absolutely key to the ministerial role at Parchmore; namely, that the minister was to be the person who above all others sought to attain, retain, and facilitate a sense of wholeness in the life and work Parchmore. Two key elements in the churches life were crucial if we were to achieve the primary objective of wholeness. These were worship and pastoral care. In the former we were constantly brought back to our roots and reminded of the wideness of God's mercy, the depth of God's concern, and in the second we were to find a way of extending the care and love of God to those who were connected with us through membership or association with the work of Parchmore.

**Worship**

One of the things that we did fairly early on in my ministry was to have a Consultation on Worship. In it we tried to gather in what people's expectations, desires and wants were. To be honest I can not remember how we did it, but remember something of the conversations that took place. Obviously what people wanted and found helpful varied enormously, and this seemed to be the fact which needed some resolution. What does it mean to worship God in such a diverse congregation of people many of whom are helped by different things!

We concluded that it meant that in an act of worship, or over a period of time members would find themselves being invited to participate in something for which they did not care. It could mean singing a traditional hymn which did not reflect their own theology, it could mean clapping hands to a modern song accompanied by guitars. Sometimes the congregation might be put into groups to explore the scriptures, sometimes silence and reflection would be the order of the day. One of the group discussing this situation said something like this: 'It means that when we are not getting what we particularly want, we rejoice that it is just what somebody else in the congregation enjoys and finds helpful'. That insight has stayed with me ever since as a most graceful way forward in congregations that encompass wide variation in taste, temperament, and maturity.

The worship area was regarded as a special place and kept for devotional use only. There was a very firm feeling that it was important that it remained so, precisely because everywhere else had been given up for youth and community use. There was something important about the essential identity of Parchmore as a Christian base of activity implicit in the determination to keep the space for worship - for worship. It was in worship that we were reminded of the spring from which the life of the church and centre emerged. It would be in worship that we were kept in the grip of the gospel.

Over the years of my ministry whilst the membership stayed roughly the same, the numbers regularly attending worship grew, and an increasing percentage were black people from Africa and the Caribbean islands. The church seats 150 people, and on a Sunday morning it would be fairly full. The evening congregation was small, numbering between ten and twenty adults. The mornings were lively, even boisterous at times, and the worship was followed by a time of fellowship over cups of coffee and soft drinks in the youth centre. I remember being impressed by the fact that parents of junior church children, and partners of members felt free to come in and share the coffee-time, even if they had not previously been to worship. There were no judgmental looks, rather a genuine pleasure at seeing them, and welcome of them. I felt this openness to others was a quality that came from the churches exposure to the neighbourhood.

**A Koinonia Time – Nurturing the 'common Life'**

Worship was the time when most of the members came together, and so it became the most important point of contact and communication. From time to time worship was focused upon issues that the work raised, or that affected our common life.

The intercessions often related to the life and work of the youth and community centre. Illustrations in preaching drew upon the experiences of our involvement in community. When the church sought to examine the issue of witnessing in a multi-faith setting, a series of evening services sought to cover the issue prayerfully, and scripturally. The same thing happened in relation to the introduction of healing services. These series could spread over a year or more.

In both morning and evening worship there was a measure of involvement of the congregation in spontaneous and informal ways. It proved almost impossible to organize participation on a rehearsal basis, but the congregation and I became more and more accustomed to conversation in worship, by in-gathering prayers, or exploring scripture passages and the theme of worship in a dialogue way.

Towards the end of my ministry I was amazed at the freedom of the congregation to respond without fuss to what they were asked to do. One morning, I felt it right that we leave the church and go downstairs into the Youth and Community Centre to say our prayers of intercession. I invited the congregation to do just that. There was no hesitation. The fit and able helped the frail, everybody gathered in a semi-circle, and made sure the elderly had chairs to sit on. We sang a song, and then prayed in the Centre for its life and work. I shall never forget it.

**Not only on a Sunday**

There was a time when we were desperate for some space for a crèche, and I asked if the rear of the church could be used. The Church Council said no. I was not pleased at the time, I had not yet then learned to fully appreciate the importance of that space to the life of the whole. But the 'no' was not a barren refusal. The Council agreed that the worship area was under-used, but felt that amidst all of the activity going on in the centre, and in a world caught up in so much frenzied activity, a place set aside for quietness, reflection, and prayer was important. If the church was under-used, then we ought to find ways of using it more for worship and for prayer.

Two initiatives grew out of this. First of all a rota was drawn up of people who would be in attendance in the church on weekday mornings. Their purpose was to supervise the building and to assist discreetly anyone who came to pray.

Secondly, we decided to have midweek worship at lunchtime every Wednesday. At first we sought to draw up a rota of people to lead this so that my 'work-load' was not increased. We were delighted and blessed by the contribution to this made by clergy and ministers of the local Anglican, Roman Catholic, and Elim Pentecostal churches. It was not very long before this time of reflective worship became a treasured part of my own devotional life. We spoke of it as an oasis in what were very often hectic and stressful times.

It was not possible to sustain the rota to keep the church open in the mornings, but the key to the church is always available in the Youth and Community Centre, and from time to time people use the place of worship, for private prayer.

**Pastoral care**

Parchmore sought as most Methodist churches do, to sustain a 'class system'. All members were put into groups of about a dozen people, and each group had a lay leader called a class leader. The leaders are expected to keep a watchful eye over their class members, and if at all possible gather them together on a regular basis for fellowship. At Parchmore some groups met, and some did not. I reckon it was to some degree a failure that we never managed to increase to a significant degree the effectiveness of this system, though we never gave up the struggle to make it work!

However, the informal networks were strong. The emphasis in class leadership terms was to encourage members to care for one another, rather than expect the class leader to do all the looking after. This reflected the stance of the minister. It was obvious at Parchmore that the minister could not possibly be the main visitor because of all the other essential duties required as minister with oversight of the whole life of the church and centre. This pastoral identity of the minister was deep within me, and it took me a long time to face up to the role change required of me.

It also seemed natural and important to cloud the distinction between those who were members of the worshipping congregation and those who were part of the life and work of the centre. As a church we assumed responsibility for pastoral care to our neighbours in the whole life of the place. As a result of wide-ranging discussions about pastoral care, Carol one of the members of the church offered herself as a Pastoral Visitor. Others were encouraged to do the same, but the few who declared an interest became extensions of the one key volunteer who did a tremendous job especially in visiting the elderly from the Pop-In and luncheon club whenever they were in hospital or any other particular need. She fought on their side in relation to a host of problems, and helped them to get the services they were entitled to, and the care they needed. She and I met most Monday lunch times, and collated the information we had from the congregation and the community work about those who were sick or facing one problem or another, and arranged for appropriate action to be taken. Our conversation always concluded with prayers for the people we had considered, and for one another, and the life of Parchmore. Carol's prayers for me and my family during those times were a regular blessing to me.

**The Church – an Inclusive Community**

I suppose the developments in worship and pastoral care indicated above both bear witness to the broadening of horizons that resulted from our involvement in community. Worship could never be a retreat from the life of the world, but it was not dominated by the world either. In worship the God who lives and suffers in and for the world was proclaimed, sought, and worshipped, and we experienced solidarity and joy in our common allegiance and in our difference. The emphasis on our corporate life and faith, and our attention to inclusive language led some to conclude that we did not value enough what is called the 'personal gospel'. We may have been too heavy on loving others and not strong enough on loving ourselves.

The Parchmore story unfolded through a period of time when charismatic renewal, and house fellowships were also breaking into the orthodox church scene. Members from Parchmore found benefit from the more extrovert manifestations of God's grace and power in these movements. Evenings of fellowship and sharing through music took place on an ecumenical basis in response to the expressed need for celebratory worship experience. But rather than promote such evenings on a narrow base of musical taste and experience they incorporated Taizé music, Wesley hymns, folk music, black Pentecostal choirs, and a wide range of contemporary Christian songs. In other words they became a celebration in and of diversity and led to a growth in relations between Christians from differing traditions, in contrast to the rather narrow theological band and style of many church worship events. The incorporation of healing services referred to earlier is another reflection of the charismatic evolution going on in the wider church setting.

Both the 'music events' and the healing services were viewed with caution and even scepticism by some of the more radical or traditional members of Parchmore, but it seemed very important that minority desires and tastes within Parchmore's constituency were able to influence the course of events and the diet of Christian celebration and ministry. It is not only in relation to unbelievers and oppressed minorities that we are called to be accepting and affirming, but also to our own brothers and sisters within the Christian community.

**Corporate body language – an evangelical sign**

Once a policy of openness and acceptance of people as they are, and in their need has been adopted it is wellnigh impossible to then impose a form of aggressive evangelism upon people, and that is even more the case when hospitality is being offered to people who are already committed to God through another faith culture. It took a long time for people who were not of the church to use the centre with confidence, knowing that they would not be pressured to take on board our beliefs about God and Jesus. That confidence was hard won.

But it would be a mistake to think that we did not want to share our faith, or that we failed to have dialogue with all kinds of people in all kinds of places. The opposite was the case. Our involvement with others, our sharing of the problems and concerns of others endeared many previously alienated from the church to it, and presented numerous opportunities to confess our faith. Our intention and hope was that the life of the Church, and the love expressed through our work and our commitments would speak for itself of the faith and the values we held. As workers we were conscious that we were not only custodians of the disciplines of community development work, but we were also accountable to the gospel in the way we dealt with people and conducted our affairs. We were serving the Lord in the serving of our neighbours, and expecting to be challenged and surprised by new revelations of God's truth and grace. We were growing together.

Throughout Parchmore's story there has been a continuous commitment to open youth work. The story charted indicates various transitions as changes took place and things happen within the social setting of the young people we were working with. Club work was never abandoned, though it went through some lean times. It is not my intention to record in detail the day-to-day events that describe the running of an open youth centre, nor to elaborate on the possible effects of that work. But I do want to at least suggest that the very fact that there was always a place in Thornton Heath for young people, black and white, from the late 'sixties to the end of the 1980s, and that in that space there were committed and caring adults willing to address the problems young people were facing, cannot have been vain labour. In some ways I have always thought it the most Christian of our commitments simply because it was work done in faith and hope and love, for which there were few thanks, many risks, and many commitments to others.

I want to focus on two things which are illustrated in the evolution of youth work and are a direct consequence of the developmental approach taken in all of Parchmore's working style.

- the gradual elimination of old territorial boundaries within Parchmore,
- the extension of the work from a centre base into the neighbourhood and town.

**Whose place is it anyway?**

Retaining a commitment to young people in a Church and Community setting provides a kind of acid test for one's ideals. Young people can be noisy and 'lively' and the young people using the youth centre were no exception.

The story of youth work was not without its dramas and difficulties sufficient to stretch the goodwill and test the coping abilities of a church and community centre.

The territory of the club was clearly designated and adhered to when I arrived. The interconnecting doors between what was called the youth centre and other parts of the building were kept firmly closed whenever the club was open. Church and community groups were able to use the youth area when the club was not open, the young people of the youth club were kept very much to their own bit of the building. This was a clear indicator that many people felt pretty insecure about getting too close to the young people. They were a bit afraid of what might happen if the young people were 'let loose' in the other parts of the premises.

From 1977–1989 there was a steady erosion of the original territorial boundaries within the Centre, which led to a much more flexible use of the accommodation. It was through taking on new work and learning from the experience that the frontiers of territory were pushed back.

### The School-Leavers Workshop

When unemployment was peaking in 1979 Alan Holdsworth was the youth worker, and he was eager to help those young people most likely to experience difficulty in getting work when they left school. Alan made contact with local secondary schools and discussed with them the possibility of running a course of training which would help school-leavers to adapt to the adult environment of competing for jobs or claiming their dole money. The schools were particularly interested in the course if Easter-leavers were aimed at. These were the early-leavers who would not be taking examinations.

Pupils from the schools were able to volunteer for the workshop. The programme lasted for a week of school-time and sought to help the young people become more aware of what they wanted to do once they had left school, teach them some skills in handling job interviews, inform them about their rights under benefit legislation, and where they could get help and advice. The course was designed by the youth worker, and was staffed by him and a student from Avery Hill College who was on placement to Parchmore at the time.

The workshop went well, and some of the young people dropped into the centre for years afterwards, and kept us up to date about their working life. There was no doubt about the worthwhile nature of the exercise, but the hassle it caused having a lively group of young people around during the day was a severe disincentive to repeating the exercise. It highlighted the fact that the space which had begun as a youth centre was not now exclusively for young people, and regular day-time users did not take kindly to finding boisterous teenagers 'disturbing their peace'.

**The Anti-Boredom scheme**

Alan Holdsworth again was the worker who came up with the idea of an Anti-Boredom Scheme. It was a programme of activities aimed at young people during the summer holiday period. The first of these schemes was launched in the summer of 1982, following discussions with a number of interested parties and financed by the local authority. The activities included art, drama, music, outdoor events, trips, and a short camping holiday. The scheme was staffed by the full-time youth worker, and a number of paid workers recruited from the local community and colleges. The activities were publicized throughout the Centre and the local neighbourhood.

The scheme was declared a success. The police testified to an improvement in community relations and a drop in crime; the youth workers involved had a concentrated experience of teamwork and of working with young people in a more intensive way. New contacts were made with young people of the neighbourhood, and new liaisons were made with the resources around us, e.g., the parks, and swimming baths. It became part of the Parchmore summer scene and three years later was a borough-wide event.

The School-leavers Workshop and the Anti-Boredom Scheme compelled the staff to consult more carefully about sharing the premises so that friction between sectional interests could be kept to a minimum and deal with frustrations openly. We were beginning to learn how important it was to pursue our own areas of work with a mind very much on the needs of others. These experiences were preparing us for the more systematic teamwork that was to come, as well as moving back the traditional frontiers of territory that had characterized Parchmore up till then.

**From an Old Principle to a New One**

The final embodiment of the new openness to flexible use of the building, and the end of the old territorial boundaries came during the time when Andy Lyons was the full-time worker in 1986. He brought a proposal to the Church Council which specifically asked for permission to develop a programme of regular weeknight activities using the rooms most suitable in the building. He had made sure that his proposals would not displace the existing users. The meeting listened carefully, asked some questions, and then passed the proposal unanimously and wished the youth worker the best of luck and God's blessing! He could hardly believe it, and I must say I was somewhat surprised that the new principle met with virtually no resistance. Minds had certainly moved, but so had the people. Many of those now sitting on the Church Council were new, and did not feel bound to the decisions of their forebears. The days of defensiveness and of protecting space had lessened, and the developments in the work and our understanding of what it meant to share had increased. It was now all right, not only for the elderly to use the youth centre for their lunch club, but also for the youth club to use the space formerly denied them in the rest of the building.

### Beyond Parchmore into Neighbourhood and Town

#### *Green Lane Estate*

This is a serial story. I picked up the results of Garth's labours with the youth work team. They had succeeded in getting a Boys' Club to be a partner with Parchmore with the intention of leasing from the local authority a pavilion situated in a recreation ground. The pavilion was the only existing building on the estate that could have been used for youth and community provision.

Unfortunately the Boys' Club dropped out of any leasing commitment, and Parchmore was left to fight the cause alone, aided and abetted by the youth service. Before any deal could be struck the local authority decided to allocate the playing fields and the pavilion to a Trades Union.

We kept up our involvement on the estate working with some parents (mainly mums) in running a summer play scheme, and setting up a children's club in the local junior school. But we had to face the fact that we did not have the time or resources to make a significant impact. Discussions took place between ourselves, the Youth Service, the neighbourhood's Social Services team, and the local police. Our observations and all known data pointed to the need for a worker based upon the estate. We assembled our arguments and made a bid to the local authority.

A detached youth work project was initiated. We imagined that the worker would have the time and skill to involve local people in the development of the project. For a number of reasons this did not happen. First, the area designated for the worker to operate in was too large. Second, I think it was a mistake to appoint a lone worker even though he was offered more support than he took. Thirdly, there were differences of opinion about the effectiveness of the worker. In the event, very little benefit to the residents accrued. The failure of this venture remains a disappointment to me, but I still believe that the approach was right, and it remains a good illustration of Parchmore's influence and involvement in the life of Thornton Heath.

**Links with a local school**

The Lady Edridge High School for Girls was one of the local secondary schools in Thornton Heath. It got its name from the days of pre-comprehensive education. It was not a posh school, and like most of the schools in the north of the borough was multi-racial, and multi-faith. It also had to put up with the cultural myth of its more glorious past, when it was reputed to have been for nice young ladies!

Mrs Andy Blows, the school's counsellor, was a member of Parchmore Youth Club Management Committee and keen to build links between Parchmore and the school. I was a regular visitor to assemblies and sharer in the school's life. Students from the school came on placements to Parchmore, assisting in our various community work activities. Mrs Blows wanted to introduce group work as an educational method in the social studies curriculum. This desire was shared with the Parchmore staff, three of whom were trained in group work skills. A group work programme developed involving the Parchmore staff.

Each worker was assigned to meet with a group of students over the period of one term. Their first tasks were to establish group cohesion and generate an atmosphere of confidence amongst the members. The basic aims were to enable the students to determine their own agenda for discussion and/or action, and through the process of managing the group life together learn about listening, co-operation, decision-making, and how to share their ideas.

The kinds of issues that commonly emerged were not surprising, relations with parents, brothers and sisters, uncles and aunts, boy and girl friends. Religions, and matters relating to the occult were common too. Discussions often had their starting point in the heroes and heroines of pop music, films or sport. The multi-racial encounters around this quite wide range of relationship issues were deeply informative for me as worker, and often it was clear that we had created a situation in which the Hindu, Moslem, white and black British teenagers were listening to each other for the first time, and beginning to appreciate the reasons for their varying customs. There were times when the girls shared experiences that were very painful, on such occasions the group were able sometimes to offer sympathy and support, at other times they could not cope and follow-up pastoral support had to be arranged.

It was not easy to gain the atmosphere of trust, and the degree of listening that we sought in these groups. In the early stages the groups were usually dominated by two or three more precocious members competing with each other, and sometimes an embarrassed or stubborn silence. These presented different problems for the worker and the group to manage, but usually groups achieved a growing sense of confidence and ability to participate.

In groups like these, the worker is providing a very different leadership style from that which is usually experienced in the classroom, and the pupils are being given a greater responsibility for the content of the curriculum and their own behaviour. Couple those things with the kind of skills and conversations indicated above, and there does seem to be an argument for a much wider use of such experience and methods within formal education, because of the potential for learning that they contain. It is also true to say that the relationship between worker/leader and the members of the group were valued by most of the participants.

But what has all this to do with Christian ministry? My own view is that I was involving myself, as was the Parchmore staff, with an important institution of the local neighbourhood, whose influence on and responsibility for young people is important. The school was doing its best to provide opportunities for young people in a multi-racial setting, and from a variety of backgrounds to develop skills and explore attitudes to one another and to life, which would have significant impact upon their future, and the future climate of the communities they live in. As a minister I cared about the same things. I think that the programme outlined above gave us an opportunity to be part of the community's and the local authorities educational team. We were making a distinctive contribution, sharing our own experience and insights. We all experienced something of what it means to work together with young people in a plural setting on things that mattered to them. I never doubted during the time I was involved that this was fulfilling for me as a minister, and enabled me to be in touch with the experiences and attitudes of young people. It was a genuine opportunity to relate with young people who may otherwise never get to know a Christian minister, never experience in however limited a form the concern we as a church had for them. A survey of the pupils responses to these sessions encouraged those engaged in the process to believe that educational and pastoral benefits were being grasped by at least one-third of the pupils!

The Lady Edridge High School for Girls was closed as part of the local authorities reorganization plans, but the development of the group work programme was extended into other schools through the collaboration of the Youth and Education services.

*Parchmore and the London Borough of Croydon*
The reader will have noted that a great deal of Parchmore's work is done in collaboration with other agencies, and not least with the London Borough of Croydon. The fact that the Youth Service was as committed to community development as we were enabled that co-operation to be particularly fruitful.

Like my predecessors Garth Rogers and George Lovell, I was part of the Borough's training team for part-time workers, and much involved in developing strategies for youth work which took real account of young people's needs. The extended colleagueship which I enjoyed with officers, councillors, and youth workers was a setting in which my vocation as a minister was never disguised, often challenged, and valued. I was enriched by my wide association and this in turn contributed to my contribution in church circles. A by-product of this broad ministry was that Parchmore's profile was kept in view, and seen for the most part as a good investment of tax-payers money!

*Parchnore's choice – Not either or but both*
This section has given nearly all its space to the open youth work, and it would be misleading and unfair not to bear witness to the work of the uniformed organizations. The Guides, Brownies and Boys' Brigade have continued to operate alongside the open youth work, providing a different kind of opportunity for children and young people to enjoy themselves, and learn new skills in various categories, and the common social skill of working and playing

together in a multi-racial, Christian context. For the most part these organizations have catered for children of church families and their friends.

The dedication of their leaders has been outstanding over the years, not only in an organizational sense, but in terms of pastoral care. The children and young people in these groups have been able to make a fantastic contribution to the life of the church, sharing fully in its worship, and its communal life. The cherishing of the children in the church was a beautiful thing, and experiencing them at play and so much at ease within Parchmore's life was impressive.

Devotees to different styles of youth work can often be quite blind to the virtues of one another. The potential for sniping sometimes became a reality. It was always difficult to bring the leadership from the various sections together, though it was done from time to time. Meetings were arranged for both formal discussion, and for social occasions, and these were usually fruitful. We believed that it was important to retain a variety of provision in a neighbourhood with such diverse needs, and in a church which was committed to Christian nurture as well as offering opportunity, friendship and support to young people often estranged from church life. Maybe too often churches make a decision in terms of either /or, Parchmore chose both.

# 4. MANAGING PARCHMORE

If you have read the book up to this point, you will be conscious of a great range of work, and an impression of Parchmore as a hive of industry, housing lots of different groups, and different people. You may well be wondering how the workers survived, how was some control maintained, how was so diverse a community of believers and actors held together as a cohesive, and joyful community? Well of course it was not a cohesive, joyful community all of the time. At times it was an enormous struggle, but it is fair to say that for the most part, those who have shared the life of Parchmore look upon it as a privilege and a joy – an experience of life lived to the full, with its share of tears and laughter.

The Church Council remained the managing trustees of Parchmore Church, Youth and Community Centre. Apart from the youth worker, the staff were employed by the Church Council; all major decisions concerning taking on new staff were taken by them; and any significant developments in the work were sanctioned by them. In other words, there was no confusion about where ultimate authority lay for the project as a whole. Elsewhere in this book the formation and re-formation of groups to manage the youth and community work has been recorded, the evolution of structures continued during the years 1977 –1989.

In this section I will tell of the ways we sought to keep ourselves whole, and managed the workers and the work, beginning with myself.

## MANAGING MINISTER – WITH MANY HATS

The complexity of the minister's job meant that I had to try and fill many different roles: leader of worship, pastor in chief, chairperson of various committees, and colleague to the workers. Liaison officer in relation to the local authority and other agencies, and money-raiser for various projects. Development worker in local community, and teacher in church. Student and trainer in the field of youth and community work. Circuit minister, husband, father, and son... the potential for confusion, exhaustion and chaos is obvious. Parchmore folk-lore testifies to most of its previous ministers flirting with what is now known as 'burn out'. The fact that the same happened to me in my ninth year only serves to emphasize the need to take seriously ministerial support. I share now what I found to be helpful in keeping body and soul together, and retaining a creative edge to my work.

*The Job Description* was an enormous help, because it identified what the church regarded as fundamental to my role and function, and that was to be the one who above all others was to ensure the integrated nature of Parchmore. The minister was singled out as the one who alone had access to, and experienced all the areas of work. I was charged not with doing everything, but of working to ensure that the essentials of ministry were to be fulfilled through and with others. The ministry was set in the context of neighbourhood and town, which meant that I need not feel guilty about attending meetings in the Town Hall, or helping in the training of youth and social workers. The job description was a liberating document, and also one which enabled me to identify a unifying concept, that of working for wholeness within Parchmore, and in relation to the neighbourhood and town. I identified the biblical link with the New Testament role of a bishop; one who was the focus of unity in an expanding, various organization called the early church, which emerged as a result of the acts of the apostles and believers.

*Training* was laid on as part of my conditions of accepting the post as minister. The distinctive nature of the task was appreciated by the church, and the connections with Avec, and Revd Dr. George Lovell had been maintained. I was expected to attend a basic ten-day training course early in my ministry, and it proved to be a unique experience because it was obviously tailor-made for the Parchmore situation. This commitment by the church to the ongoing training of its minister was not limited to the first year. I was never refused money or permission to continue my education and personal development. It was another way in which the church demonstrated its support, and its commitment to the work. This forward thinking was also reflected in the Croydon circuit, which gave its willing support to my further training.

*A Local Community-Development Group* was formed in Croydon at the initiative of Revd Howard Mellor, a ministerial colleague in the same Methodist circuit. Parchmore's community worker, Diana

Morrison, and its youth worker, Peter Miller and the Principal Youth Officer for Croydon's youth service with myself completed the initial membership. Though its membership changed, the group continued in existence from 1979 until 1989. It was a meeting of workers in church and community who were committed to the discipline of working to community development ideals and methods. At each meeting one of the member's work situations would be focused upon, and submitted to constructive analysis. The object of the exercise was to help one another to think through the difficulties facing them, and search for ways to proceed in a developmental way. We also sought to identify principles of good practice.

The group met at six to eight week intervals, and each session allowed space for just being together before we settled down to work, because we acknowledged that the group also functioned as a support to us all. The group's work method was modelled upon the work paper sessions employed and developed by Avec.

The format we aimed to follow was as follows, though the starting time differed:

Meet at 9.30 a.m. Coffee and socializing till 10.00 Follow-up to previous session, picking up any matters that required following up, checking out progress and identifying any learning points in relation to theory and good practice.

10.45–12 noon Main Work paper. During this period one of the group presented a detailed description of a piece of work she or he was engaged in. A critical conversation during which the issues were teased out, the problems identified, and possible courses of action explored and examined.

12.00 Set agenda for next session. members were free to make a bid for the group's time and help. This included a commitment to prepare a presentation for the main work session.

Another important aspect of this group was the willingness of its members to come together at any time if one of its members was in urgent need of consultation. The members of the group were always key people in their respective organizations, and to have this facility for regular consultation, and access to the same in an emergency was a most valuable resource.

***Personal non-managerial supervision*** is a facility commonly used in the fields of youth, community and social work, and is often misunderstood by those who are not familiar with it, or who are used to the same phrase say in an industrial context. I can remember working on an assembly line in a factory one vacation and regularly having my unsatisfactory work sent back, to be done again, by my line supervisor. Against that background, supervision seems to be the duty of an overseer acting on behalf of senior management. That is not what is meant here. What I was seeking through personal supervision was time with someone who had a good understanding of my work, an interest in my personal development and well-being as a person with family and friends; somebody who could help me to work well and stay healthy in body, mind and spirit.

The person who came to mind was a United Reformed minister, and it so happened he was looking for the same kind of person for himself. We agreed to try supervising one another. We met and still meet at regular intervals. We give $1^{1}/_{4}$ hours of attention to each other, with a break in the middle for refreshment, lunch or coffee depending on the time of day. It has been so valuable to have a confidante, who knows the nature of the work I am engaged in, who is a keen reflective thinker capable of exploring the links between faith and practice, and who cares about me. The fact that in our case we have been able to offer the same kind of service to one another has brought the added bonus of mutuality to the relationship.

### MANAGING THE WORKERS – TEAMWORK

The staff team assembled itself over a period of years as the work expanded. In 1977 there were three full-time workers at Parchmore, the youth worker, community worker, and myself. In addition there was some secretarial assistance for the youth worker, and a caretaker who lived on the premises who did limited hours cleaning, opening up and locking up premises. By 1987 there were six full-time workers. How did this come about?

In 1978, Carol Dobbs a member of the church, mother of two small children and part of the Mums and Toddlers group, and a helper in the Brownies became the part-time secretary to the youth worker. Carol soon added hours of voluntary labour to her paid sessions, and it was clear that in addition to her secretarial skills she worked well with people, was a great receptionist and very good listener. Year by year we managed to add more paid hours and she eventually became a full-time member of staff, serving not only the youth worker, but the centre as a whole.

In 1985 we were prevailed upon to accept two young women from a Youth Training Scheme on placement at Parchmore. One disappeared almost as soon as she came, but the other Nicola Hill took to the work and Parchmore's lifestyle like a fish to water. When her three months placement came to an end she asked if she could extend her time with us to six months. At the end of six months she asked for a job!

It so happened that her request coincided with a request from the local authority that Parchmore take over the management and servicing of a Good Neighbour scheme and lunch club which was based nearby, off Thornton Heath High Street. Funding was available to employ a worker for twenty hours a week. The job included administering the Good Neighbour scheme, and the lunch club, but it was also hoped that there could be further development of both premises and the work with the elderly people living adjacent in two high rise blocks of flats, and with a small mother and baby group.

Discussion took place rather hurriedly amongst the staff, and with the appropriate church committees and Nicola was added to the group of paid workers. Nicola, like Carol before her did more hours work than she was paid for, and as money became available she too became full-time.

The extra money for these extensions to the staff came from increased grant allocation from the local authority. But it must be confessed that we were not able to pay any of the staff what they were worth at this time. The developments in the work, and the impact of Parchmore in the local community and the borough, were sacrificially gained through the dedication of these workers.

Last but not least, the employment of the caretaker by the church moved from a part-time to a full-time appointment, but slowly! The caretaker in residence in 1977 was a widow, whose age made it difficult for her to do the job. The flat was the last home she had shared with her husband, and she needed the companionship that Parchmore supplied, and the place she occupied within its corporate life. Eventually, alternative accommodation was found and it was possible to think of the caretaking role afresh.

Over the succeeding years three caretakers were employed. The last of them was appointed as full-time worker in 1986. A decision which cost the church an extra £2,000 per annum at the time, but which at last recognized that it was necessary to service and support the workers and the work by providing the resources to keep the buildings clean and tidy, and respond quickly to the maintenance and repair jobs. Two of the three people who became caretaker during this period were church members, committed to the work we were doing, and the kind of church we were trying to be. One had been with us on placement from Avery Hill College, and was finding it difficult to get a job in youth and community work. The second retired from the police force in order to serve the church full-time.

The commitment of these people was extremely high, their abilities expanded along with the demands of the work, and their personal relations deepened.

Recruiting staff from amongst one's own ranks, and from the local community can be cosy and safe. On the other hand it would be strange if an organization committed to the community development approach did not produce organic growth! What is certain is that the minister, and the community work section stayed together for nearly ten years and so achieved a high degree of trust and mutual support. The commitment of these people was extremely high, their abilities expanded along with the demands of the work, and their personal relationships deepened.

The work was becoming more and more complex which meant that the good relations needed to be augmented by appropriate good practice. Our life together was also punctuated every three years or so by the accommodation of a new youth worker into the team, as one worker was replaced by another. There were four of them during the years of my ministry and each of them stimulated our thinking, and contributed to our development as a whole.

Members of staff also benefited from in-service training, participated in the local community development group referred to on page 165f, and were encouraged to have the kind of non-managerial supervision which I described earlier in relation to my own support and development. The fact that we worked in many other settings both church and non-church, meant that our own agendas were changing often, and our programmes evolving out of collaborative processes with various groups of people. These devices and our very live involvement with the local community meant that our problem was not stagnation or boredom, but coping with the number of ideas and demands that were generated.

**Teamwork – Collaboration and so much more**

Andy Lyons was the third youth worker to join the team, and he it was who challenged me to face up to the fact that I was not simply a colleague, but a team leader; that we were not just a group of people working in the same place and in friendly relationships, but that we were having to work with each other in a very complex set-up. We needed to find working practices and a discipline that ensured that difficulties real and potential were dealt with. This transition could be described as moving from collaboration to teamwork.

The impact of acknowledging our need to work together as a team was very important. We were not starting out as strangers, and there was a measure of trust between us, we had some idea of what each other did and who we were responsible to. Most of all we shared a common purpose. We tried to communicate with one another, and cover for one another, and help one another, but these arrangements were assumed, and not negotiated, and often did not work well. Whenever there was stress and tension between us, or in the centre, a failure in communication would be one of its causes! And I mean not only communication of information, but communication as a human interaction, a lack of sensitivity, a failure to read the signs, a failure in love.

Adopting our identity as a team, meant that we gave time to clarifying our respective roles and that clarified and sharpened up our job descriptions. We set times for meeting regularly together. We tried to meet every fortnight, and sometimes this was really hard to fit in. It is especially difficult for the community work staff, because well-laid plans are so easily devastated by an unexpected withdrawal of voluntary help, or an emergency with someone they work with. It sometimes felt like the team came second and the work came first, but I think that was more to do with the circumstances of the work situation than a fair reflection of how people felt.

The team also had 'away days', when we got away from Parchmore, usually to a nearby Youth Centre where we were provided with friendly and generous hospitality, a quiet room to work in, and resources of flip charts, etc. Sometimes we used an outside worker to facilitate our discussions, especially when we were reviewing our work, or re-defining our objectives.

We tried to nurture the life of the team, by having time-off together. The occasional lunch, or day-out, when we simply enjoyed one another and relaxed in each others company.

By a series of building modifications we were eventually provided with more spacious and comfortable office accommodation, which allowed three workers to work in one room. These alterations coincided with the transition to teamwork and were an important contribution to its development. We had always thought it was important that the church and community at large were able to see that we worked together in order to endorse the holistic nature of Parchmore. The pleasant working conditions were a far cry from the pokey rooms we had occupied, and did much to boost the morale. It is obvious, but not always appreciated and acted upon, but the place we provide for people to work in speaks volumes about how we value them or do not.

Day-by-day we tried to engineer a lunch break, again not always possible. One of the problems was that the work schedules of youth worker, community worker and minister do not always marry very well. But setting an objective of a lunch break did increase the frequency of our times of communication, and meant that we kept in touch with one another as people as well as colleagues. We were often working under lots of pressure, and our efforts were not always appreciated by those we worked for and with. The lunch break was something like a staff room in a school must be when Form 3B has driven the teacher round the bend. A place of humour, and of support, minor explosions and expletives, a place to scream and laugh!

This book is written as story rather than a training manual, so there is only passing reference to the theory and practice of team-building, development, and consolidation. It is important however to record that the transition to teamwork was not only the result of a change of consciousness, but also meant the acquisition of a new set of skills, and commitment to a new set of disciplines.

In conclusion, I feel that the teamwork approach is the most satisfactory structure to embody the holistic approach to the work of the centre. The experience of it also proved to be one of the most satisfying and rewarding of my life so far!

## MANAGING THE WORK

### The Community Council

The Community Council met at least four times a year, and provided space within the life of the Centre for the various groups and organizations to meet one another, air grievances, and deal with the internal organization of booking rooms, etc. It was also the only body to which the community worker reported, and it sanctioned any decisions that had been made with regard to funds held in the account, including the wages bill; though this was so discreetly handled that nobody really knew what the workers were getting paid!

The Council was struggling, in that the meetings were often poorly attended, and those who did come were often motivated by the need to complain, or to make a concerted request for extra space for their activity. The Council was most effective as a point of communication. The Community Worker could share news concerning any new groups or any new opportunities that were emerging for volunteering; the collective enterprises of Bazaar, and Community Concert were discussed and encouraged in the Council. Individual groups shared their own news and views. From time to time issues thrown-up in the neighbourhood could be discussed.

But there was a growing sense of unease about the appropriateness of the constitution, and in 1980 a new one was put together via a process of suggestions, drafts and amendments over a series of Council meetings. It represents the way the Council saw itself at the time.

*Item 3 read:* The Council shall be a delegated body of Parchmore Road Methodist Church Council, hereafter referred to as the Church Council.

*Item 4 read:* The duties of the Council shall be:

(a) to receive details of new user-organizations from the Church Council or Property Committee.

(b) to welcome new organizations to Parchmore with a letter of welcome, an invitation to select their representative on the Council, a copy of the Council's constitution, a copy of the minutes of the previous meeting, and an information pack giving details of all Parchmore organizations and the procedure for room bookings;

(c) to maintain an up-to-date register of all user organizations and their contact person;

(d) to make an annual up-date of the information pack described in (b)

(e) to arrange for each meeting of the Council to receive a verbal report of the activities of one or more of the user organizations;

(f) to include an item on the agenda of each meeting for the discussion of any problems that may have occurred in the shared use of the Parchmore premises, or within organizations;

(g) to promote and organize events in which all user organizations can participate in working or fund-raising together;

(h) to take such actions, including the initiation of new community activities as it deems appropriate for the furtherance of community work in the Thornton Heath neighbourhood and to make recommendations and proposals to other bodies;

(i) to act as banker for the financing of the work of the Council, and any project for which the Council takes responsibility.

The duties of the Parchmore Road Church Council

This extract gives an indication of the functions the Community Council was meant to fulfil, and it is clear that a main reason for its continuing existence was to maintain lines of communication within the life of the Centre as a whole. However there was no significant improvement in attendance. We had some very precious moments, but they were shared by only a few.

Part of the problem was that as the Centre grew in size and complexity the full-time staff dealt with many of the problems that had previously been handled by the committee. The 'office' became the centre of communications, and particularly Carol in the office! It was not possible to wait for the cycle of church meetings to deal with day-to-day matters of maintenance and organization. The centre ran on a day-by-day, week-by-week basis not a quarterly one! Gradually some of the functions of the committee were transferred to the office.

Another major factor was that the Council was not an appropriate body to manage the employment of the staff, or manage the community work programme. It took us some time to acknowledge this fact, and when we did we had to work at the next evolution in the structures of Parchmore – the formation of a Community Work Management Committee.

**Community Work Management Committee**

Our first attempt at this task failed abysmally! We assembled a group of people who were sympathetic to the work, and who represented various interests in the life of Parchmore. The trouble was they were not experienced in managing, nor were they skilled enough in community work to be a real help to the workers. So much had to be explained about the work each time we met that instead of being a support to the workers and a help in decision-making, it simply added to the burdens of very busy people.

When it became obvious that it was not working we scrapped it and started again, and tried to identify more clearly what we needed. The second attempt was much more successful, but still very hard work to conceive and establish.

A small group was appointed by the Church Council to work with the community work staff to identify as precisely as we could what the objectives and functions of a management committee should be. Community workers can be very defensive about being managed, and Parchmore's were no exception! They had after all been used to working under the supervision of the minister, and were confident about the support and understanding they received. They also experienced a good deal of misunderstanding about the way they worked and sometimes people in the church said things which undermined the good relations they tried so hard to maintain with and between all the users of the centre.

It became evident that we had to seek out a group of people who understood and endorsed the underlying beliefs and philosophy of community work. They would need to be capable of offering personal support, and firmly assisting the formation of policy in consultation with the staff. The group would need to have the confidence of the Church Council, and the church would have to be represented on it. One of the objectives was that the Management Committee would report regularly to the Church Council and be advocates of the community work. Until this time this had been done by the workers themselves or the minister.

The formation of the Community Work Management Committee as a delegated body of the Church Council institutionalized the work firmly within the structure of Parchmore. It became less dependent on who the minister was. In spite of all that had been done and achieved at Parchmore there was still a sense of vulnerability about the work. We were conscious that very few of the original 'Ten Centre' churches had survived, and none had developed so fully as at Parchmore. Interaction with the circuit over ministerial appointments had indicated that there was still a lot of power in the hands of people who did not really understand the nature of Parchmore in community development terms. It was a necessary part of the evolution of the work that responsibility for it be transferred from a personal to a corporate base.

Securing this constitutional base also meant we gave time to the long overdue task of instituting and renewing contracts of employment and getting some employment practices in place. The period of trust, personal relations, and the collective commitment of the pioneers was to give way to these necessary management structures and practices. I hoped that they could be put in place without losing the edge of commitment and loyalty to one another and the cause which had served to bond those involved up to this point in time.

The members of the Management Committee were drawn from the church, the Croydon Guild of Voluntary Organizations, the Youth Service and Croydon Social Services Community Development section. They were people who were friends of Parchmore, thoroughly committed to its work, and with a lot of skills for the task, they also had the trust and confidence of the staff. There was a discussion in the Church Council during which it became evident that some members wanted the church to have a controlling influence (i.e. a working majority) on the committee, but the proposed constitution was agreed without amendment to the levels of representation.

**Incorporating new groups**

As a Christian centre we believed that the way we handled relationships with all who crossed the threshold was important. Day by day we hoped to disclose the essence of our faith in our actions and responses to others. The treatment they received was the litmus paper by which we would be judged.

*First Impressions Are Important!* When someone asks if they can rent a room, they may have already had a few rebuffs. They may have inquired with the local authority and other churches and not had a very sympathetic response. So when we say that we want to meet and talk with them about their ideas they are often very apprehensive. They may suspect that they are going to be submitted to criticism or an evangelical assault!

The initial meeting is usually with the minister and one member of staff, in a small room with the usual courtesies of hospitality. It is important to treat people well and to take their ideas and ambitions for community action seriously and sympathetically. It is just as vital that a group meeting at Parchmore realizes what it is getting itself into, and that it wants to be part of it. So it is that we shared with all prospective new groups the ideals, and beliefs that undergird all of our work, and invited them to participate in the Community Council and corporate life.

We could not always give people what they wanted. But we always tried to help them find the next step forward, sharing our knowledge of community work and the neighbourhood to help them on.

It was not unusual for our initial meetings to have a pastoral and therapeutic dimension. We all know of people who having suffered pain or loss are fired with the desire to do something to help others who endure similar circumstances. I remember a woman who wanted to start up a yoga class. Pain was written in her features and we were moved by her account of her sufferings and of the help yoga had been in her recovery. We were not able to give her what she was looking for in terms of a room at certain times of the week, but none of us felt the time together was anything but precious, and maybe she got something more precious than she asked for.

If a group became part of Parchmore it did so knowing that it was a Christian organization intent upon working with others and God to create a community which offers care for the vulnerable, and liberty from racism, sexism and ageism. They knew we were genuinely interested in receiving what they had to offer to that process, and that we were willing to share with them the resources we had. There is no doubt that this approach to newcomers contributed greatly to the shaping of Parchmore's life. So often the volunteers and community activists we welcomed became incorporated into the life of the centre from these careful beginnings.

***Sharing the costs and helping one another.*** Many and various are the groups that meet at Parchmore. A Dance School has met on a Saturday for many years providing an income for its teachers as well as an opportunity for all ages to enjoy the pleasure and discipline of dance. At the other end of the scale SANDS was a small support group for parents whose child had died before, during or shortly after birth. In between are groups of all sizes and kinds. We were often asked 'How much do groups pay?' And we replied, 'It depends...'

It has long been established that to use the building in the spirit of the gospel the strong have to support the weak and anything as crude as a tariff applied to all without discrimination just will not suffice. This theological approach to charges made to groups was made clear at the beginning. I never heard any objections to it. It was of course messy, and requires a review system so that when small groups become large or vice versa charges are amended. But it is important that the financial system reflects the beliefs of the organization.

**Corporate events**

We sought to encourage a community spirit by organizing events to which all the groups from Parchmore were invited to contribute. Through these events we hoped to give substance and character to our corporate existence.

***The Community concert.*** This was an annual event organized by the community worker. The formula was straight forward; every group in the church, youth and community sections was invited to present an item at a variety concert. Not all groups responded positively, but enough did, and the result was an evening in which something of the essence of Parchmore was in evidence; people of all ages, tastes, ability and cultures combined to make a thoroughly enjoyable evening. Those who took part, and many who came experienced a sense of belonging, something like fun, but more like joy.

I never ceased to be impressed by the large number of nice people that were involved in the life of Parchmore. Usually we saw them separately in their different roles and settings, to see them together was often overwhelming. I thanked God for them all, and was excited by their potential.

***The Bazaar.*** The Community Council encouraged the idea of corporate responsibility for the upkeep of Parchmore. The Centre was regarded as being of value to the whole community. The annual bazaar gave everyone an opportunity to raise funds for the general upkeep of the place. The bazaar had originally been organized by the church in the way bazaars usually are. It was the community worker who saw that the bazaar could be an event through which all the users of Parchmore might work together for the common good. As so often happens more and more of the organization fell upon the community worker and a loyal band of helpers. But on the day most sections from the youth and community sections and the church were involved in common cause if not always in perfect harmony!

***The sponsored swims.*** Sponsored Events of various kinds were arranged to raise funds for special projects. A number of sponsored swims were held. As with the community concert each group was challenged to provide a team, and each team got their own sponsors. A local school let us have the use of their swimming baths, and the event was organized almost entirely by swimming club enthusiasts from the church. I guess the secret here was in using the resources of place, expertise and enthusiasm that were around.

***A Royal visit.*** Once in a while something happens in the life of a place which offers an opportunity to build community. After the racial disturbances in South London we were invited to receive a visit from Princess Diana. We were not given much time to arrange this royal event, but we were in no doubt that we should use the occasion to build our common life, to promote participation.

Our motive affected our whole strategy. Every group was allocated some tickets for the occasion, each group was to decide for itself who should have them. The key groups in our race relations work were invited to arrange a presentation of their activities on the day, and space was allocated to them. We prepared a Press statement which made clear what we were trying to achieve, giving details of what happened at the centre to promote racial harmony, and we made it clear that the basis and inspiration of our work was the Christian gospel.

It was a beautiful February day, the sun shone out of a clear blue sky and the entrance to Parchmore was besieged by people. The press and TV were put in their places and warded-off when they tried to put words into our mouths. Cameras clicked and everyone involved was pleased to be there and sharing in such a happy occasion. I think they were proud too. Proud that all the hard work over the years was being recognized and that they were part of it.

There were those who refused to attend. People who thought that we were betraying our ideals of equality in playing host to the most privileged. And nobody can deny that it is galling that one can get things done because royalty is coming that you can't get done because the poor are needy. Those people who stayed away were heard and respected. But on the whole I think we made good use of the day, and it brought a lot of happiness to a lot of people and allowed us to proclaim nationally and locally that church life and community building go hand in hand.

***Annual Meetings.*** The Methodist structures encourage an annual meeting to give to the members and adherents an opportunity to discuss their ideas and concerns. We tried to ensure that these meetings reflected the scope and diversity of Parchmore as a whole. People from the youth and community work were encouraged to attend, and in the programmes we arranged we tried to focus on key aspects of our work. Our objectives in these meetings were to keep people informed about the developments taking place in Parchmore as a whole, to bring people together and encourage them to share with each other in discussion and socially (a meal was an important part of these occasions), and to help the people to raise items for consideration and action for the coming year.

Worship became an integral part of our annual meetings both to celebrate the past, remind ourselves of the vision of the Kingdom and our place within it, and to commit ourselves to our shared future. It was always important to keep worship and work connected, and to link our present to the historical process of God's saving activity. In our efforts to do this one year we dramatized some of the significant events in the evolution of Parchmore from a suburban Methodist church to a Church and Community Development Project. We told the story of how that evolution had been in response to the gospel and the changing needs of the people of Thornton Heath. People who had experienced these things first-hand were still around and it was important that their story be told and shared with those who had joined the church since.

On another AGM we had a service of testimony, when people spoke of the relationship between their personal faith and the work that they were engaged in through Parchmore. A youth worker from the Youth Club and one from the Boys' Brigade gave moving accounts of their growth in faith and commitment to Jesus through their work with young people. A Pop-In volunteer described how his life had been transformed, after his wife had died, because of the care he had been given and contribution he had been able to make. A member who had recently joined the church from Accra in Ghana described his own journey of faith and how he had found Parchmore. He expressed his appreciation of the cosmopolitan nature of the congregation, and challenged us all to be far more bold in our response to prayers in worship. He wanted to hear some Amens as if we really meant them!

In the content and conjunction of worship and AGM's we were seeking to maintain the holistic outlook, to affirm our history and faith, and remind ourselves of the beliefs out of which the life of worship and action flows. I suppose it was our way of embodying the sense of continuity and of development.

Over the years we also moved towards producing an annual report which was supposed to be available to the congregation two weeks before that AGM. It was hoped that this would encourage more critical participation and increase awareness. It may have done the latter but was not very successful in the former! The production of an annual report was also part of recognizing that Parchmore had become a significant voluntary organization in the

Borough which used public as well as church funds, and that it should seek to be more accountable. The annual reports were also very helpful in reminding people of our purposes and in seeking funds from trusts, etc.

After some years of this style of AGM there were complaints that the Annual Meeting was so concerned with the work of the centre that we were unable to deal with the needs and concerns of the church itself. I am not sure that this was true, in that the Church Council could set-up any meeting it wished in order to attend to its own needs. However in response to this complaint there was an attempt to limit the focus on the whole and to focus more on the church. Certainly one of the problems that we were encountering was the very thing that was present when I began my ministry at Parchmore. 'How do we balance all the work of such a various and energetic body?' I guess that question will always be present and rightly so.

# 5. HANDING OVER

Twelve years is long time for a Methodist minister to stay in one place. It is said that the itinerant system provides stimulation for ministers and the churches to which they go. I could think of no more stimulating place to be when I was asked to leave Parchmore. It is inevitable that in such a place there will always be new opportunities emerging, fresh challenges to respond to. It is just as inevitable that leaving will be a wrench when so much has been received and invested into a place and a people.

One of the features of Parchmore's development has been the insistence on the importance of continuity in ministry. Not that each succeeding minister should be a clone of her or his predecessor, but that the tradition of the church which encompasses its life and work should be honoured and built upon from generation to generation.

I had been happy to take up the inheritance when I began; the cause of the homeless young, the desire for a place for the lonely elderly, the needs of the Green Lane estate. The debate about what it meant to be a Christian centre for community life when an increasing number of neighbours came from and practised different faith cultures would continue. I had now to let my contribution and my dreams for Parchmore lie in the hands and hearts of the people and whoever would follow me as minister.

Over the years we had worked hard at institutionalizing good practice and providing systems in the life of Parchmore that would aid its future development. Knowing that I was leaving we particularly sought to ensure that the main working committees, especially the management groups of the youth and the community work sections were well equipped to provide support for the workers and the new minister. We had to do all that we could to ensure that a new minister was as aware as possible about the kind of church Parchmore was, which meant providing background information, updating the church's policy statement and minister's job description. Together with the Croydon Methodist circuit officers a selection procedure was worked out, and an induction programme prepared. All this provided work through which both I and the church and the staff began to come to terms with the awful pain of parting.

Hopefully the new minister would find Parchmore to be the invigorating experience I had found it to be, and Parchmore will continue to be a source of care and hope to the needy and a light to the world of grace, mercy and love. My last words must be to offer a tender thanks to all those who travelled the journey with me, who forgave me much, guided me often and loved me when I was up and when I was down. My thanks too to the host of people who responded to the urge within them to give spirited service to their neighbours and confirm God's liveliness in old and young bones and skins of every hue.

# The story continues

*– The Revd Stephen Mares, Minister from 1989*

1989 is the date at which this telling of the story of Parchmore comes to an end: but it certainly is not the end of Parchmore. At the time of writing, February 1993, we are in the midst of celebrating twenty-five years as a Church, Youth and Community Centre with plans for visits by each of the authors of this book, a weekend thinking about our future, plus other events to bring our whole community together.

In 1989 on Peter's departure, I became Minister of Parchmore. Within a few months twenty-five years of experience had been removed from the scene: Peter's departure coming very soon after Diana Morrison's. I arrived to discover Parchmore's Community Work moving into a new era, with advertisements already scheduled for various publications as we sought a new Senior Community Development Worker. Community Work at Parchmore had grown up, and a time of increased professionalism had dawned. Within months we, or perhaps it should be I because I was very much the learner, had learned about how to measure candidates against our declared personal specifications, interviewing by 'Equal Opportunity' procedures, and that we did not have enough money to recruit a 'Senior' worker, worthy of the name. Within a couple of months it was back to the drawing board, and shortly after a new qualified Youth and Community Worker, Miron Smith, joined the team as a Community Development Worker.

There is not the space in this tail-piece to tell much of the story of the past five years. There is really just enough to let you know that Parchmore continues and is going strong.

The membership of the Church is still just under 150, with significant numbers of new members made, replacing those dying, moving or otherwise leaving our fellowship. Congregations, numbers in Junior Church and in church attached Youth work are healthy, and we continue to reflect the mix that is Thornton Heath.

The Youth Work continues to be highly valued by the Borough, for its wide ranging and imaginative programme. Plans are once again being considered to redesign the building to suit 1990s style youth work with its emphasis on group work, inter-actions between young people and staff, and social education, Andy Winton, the latest Youth Worker in the long line is exploring this possibility, along with other ideas to improve what we can offer to all young people in the neighbourhood.

Community Work has undergone the greatest changes of recent years, facing up to many of the increasing difficulties in society, and having to take hard decisions about what it is possible to be involved with and what is not. Many of the elderly have been part of Lunch Club or Pop-In for many years: and many of the volunteers have grown old themselves. We face an increasingly elderly society as well as the desire to respond to the needs of the unemployed, the mentally ill in community, those who are homeless and in Bed and Breakfast accommodation, and the many refugees now resident, often temporarily, in Croydon. We have had to decide we cannot do everything.

It has also been an area in which we have had to become increasingly professional as the drive for 'value for money' has changed the way Local Authorities view projects such as Parchmore. Grant applications require greater detail of what is offered for the money invested; accounts are periodically inspected by Local Authority Officers; and further changes are in the pipeline. We move towards the era of Community Care Plans, of the Local Authority as purchaser of services from other providers, of entering into Contracts (or service agreements) rather than receiving Grant Aid. Increased professionalism in the way we operate has already become essential, and will become still more so.

There is a great deal more that could be said about each of the areas of work, but I am in danger of doing what we always try to avoid that is to split Parchmore into three separate enterprises. It is not. The three aspects continue to relate to each other, and there is still a strong emphasis on trying to create a sense of wholeness. We hope to find ways of enabling everyone who comes within the sphere of Parchmore to recognize that they are part of the whole.

One of the ways of doing this was the Community Concert. From 1989 this has been revised. We now have an Open Day about every eighteen months to two years, when each part of Parchmore mounts a static display to show its activities and ethos and all those who can put on some sort of entertainment or demonstration have the chance to do so. Our most recent one was attended by both local Members of Parliament, and press coverage in five different publications as well as at least five hundred visitors.

We are also into a process called 'Review and Renew' in which every aspect of the life of the Church and Centre is examined, reviewed and we hope renewed for the future. There are still issues in church life, in Youth Work and in Community Work that need to go on being addressed and above all there is the need to maintain the vision of the wholeness of what we are.

At twenty-five years on in Parchmore's story as a Church, Youth and Community Centre, there is no sitting back and resting on our laurels. Parchmore has become a vital part of the fabric of Thornton Heath, and a real centre of Community. The title of our weekend away seems as good a place as any to stop: 'Towards the next twenty-five years'.

**The Parchmore story continues.**